BIBLE STUDY COMMENTARY

Matthew

Bible Study Commentary

Matthew

GEORGE BEASLEY–MURRAY

Scripture Union
130, City Road, London EC1V 2NJ

CHRISTIAN LITERATURE CRUSADE
Fort Washington, Pennsylvania 19034

© 1984 Scripture Union
130 City Road, London EC1V 2NJ

First published 1984

ISBN 0 86201 211 2 (UK)
ISBN 0 87508 164 9 (USA)

All rights reserved. No part of this publication may be reproduced, stored in a
retrieval system, or transmitted, in any form or by any means, electronic,
mechanical, photocopying, recording or otherwise, without the prior
permission of Scripture Union

Map: Jenny Grayston

Phototypeset in Great Britain by
Input Typesetting Ltd., London SW19 8DR.

Printed in Great Britain by
Ebenezer Baylis & Son Limited
The Trinity Press, Worcester, and London.

General Introduction

The worldwide church in the last quarter of the twentieth century faces a number of challenges. In some places the church is growing rapidly and the pressing need is for an adequately trained leadership. Some Christians face persecution and need support and encouragement, while others struggle with the inroads of apathy and secularism. We must come to terms, too, with the challenges presented by Marxism, Humanism, a belief that 'science' can conquer all the ills of mankind, and a whole range of Eastern religions and modern sects. If we are to make anything of this confused and confusing world it demands a faith which is solidly biblical.

Individual Christians, too, in their personal lives face a whole range of different needs – emotional, physical, psychological, mental. As we think more and more about our relationships with one another in the body of Christ and as we explore our various ministries in that body, as we discover new dimensions in worship and as we work at what it means to embody Christ in a fallen world, we need a solid base. And that base can only come through a relationship with Jesus Christ which is firmly founded on biblical truth.

The Bible, however, is not a magical book. It is not enough to say, 'I believe', and quote a few texts selected at random. We must be prepared to work with the text until our whole outlook is moulded by it. We must be ready to question our existing position and ask the true meaning of the word for us in our situation. All this demands careful study not only of the text but also of its background and of our culture. Above all it demands prayerful and expectant looking to the Spirit of God to bring the word creatively to our own hearts and lives.

This new series of books has been commissioned in response to the repeated requests for something new to follow on from *Bible Characters and Doctrines*. It is now over ten years since the first series of Bible Study Books were produced and it is hoped the new books will reflect the changes of the last ten years and bring the Bible text to life for a new generation of readers. The series has three aims:

1. To encourage regular, systematic, personal Bible reading. Each volume is divided into sections ideally suited to daily use, and will normally provide material for three months (the exceptions being *Psalms* and *1 Corinthians-Galatians*, four months, and *Mark* and *Ezra-Job*, two months). Used in this way the books will cover the entire Bible in five years. The comments aim to give background information and enlarge on the meaning of the text, with special reference to the contemporary relevance. Detailed questions of application are, however, often left to the reader. The questions for further study are designed to aid in this respect.

2. To provide a resource manual for group study. These books do not provide a detailed plan for week by week study. Nor do they present a group leader with a complete set of ready-made questions or activity ideas. They do, however, provide the basic biblical material and, in the questions for further discussion, they give starting points for group discussion.

3. To build into a complete Bible commentary. There is, of course, no shortage of commentaries. Here, however, we have a difference. Rather than look at the text verse by verse the writers examine larger blocks of text, preserving the natural flow of the original thought and observing natural breaks.

Writers have based their comments on the Revised Standard Version and some have also used the New International Version in some detail. The books can, however, be used with any version.

Matthew: Introduction

The origin of the Gospel

The earliest statement handed down concerning the composition of Matthew's gospel is that of Papias, bishop of Hierapolis, writing in the second quarter of the second century. The historian Eusebius quotes him as saying, 'Matthew compiled the oracles in the Hebrew language, and everyone interpreted them as he was able'. Naturally that led Christians to believe that the apostle Matthew was the author of the first Gospel as it stands. A difficulty about the statement, however, is that this Gospel was manifestly not written in the language of the Jews (Aramaic) and translated into Greek, for through its whole length it reflects a use of Mark's Gospel, which was written also in Greek. If Papias was rightly informed he must have been referring to an earlier source or stage of the Gospel. This could have been the collection of teaching which is so prominent in Matthew, and which was shared by Luke, or even the collection of Old Testament 'testimonies' to Christ, which is unique to Matthew's Gospel. More likely the statement reflects a tradition that the apostle Matthew composed a draft Gospel at an early date, which was available to the evangelist who authored the Gospel as we have it, and which could have been known to Mark also. Written in Aramaic, it would have been translated into Greek, and so our present Gospel came to be written with the aid of the Greek Mark and other sources translated into that tongue (notably the teaching common to Matthew and Luke, and the collected Old Testament testimonies; the sayings found only in Matthew will largely have been in the primitive 'Gospel').

The structure of the Gospel

The most obvious difference between Matthew and Mark is Matthew's inclusion of discourses of Jesus, which occur through the body of the Gospel. Each of these ends with an identical statement: 'Now when Jesus had finished these sayings . . .' (so after chs. 5–7, 10, 13, 18, 24–25). The American scholar B.W.Bacon suggested that if the narrative sections which preceded these discourses were linked with them, we would then have a Gospel in five 'books' (chs. 3–7, 8–10, 11–13, 14–18, 19–25), preceded by an introduction (chs. 1–2) and followed by an epilogue (chs. 26–28); the Gospel would then correspond in structure to the five books of the Law, the five books of Psalms and of Proverbs, the Jewish grouping of the 'Rolls' (Ruth, Song of Solomon, Lamentations, Ecclesiasticus, Esther) and other similarly structured late Jewish works; Matthew composed his Gospel to commend it as word of God to the Jewish people. It is a brilliant notion, but reluctantly we have to discount it, or at least to tame it. A Gospel is, as one has put it, a passion narrative with an extended introduction; you cannot have a presentation of the Gospel of Christ in which the story of the death and resurrection of the Lord is viewed as an addendum, or even a mere 'finis'. Moreover ch. 23 should not be grouped with chs. 24–25 as one discourse, as many would have it; Matthew has *six* discourses, and possibly ch. 11 should be viewed as a seventh.

More simply, it has been observed that the phrase, 'from that time Jesus began to. . .' (in 4:17 and 16:21), is all but unique to Matthew and it occurs at key points in his Gospel. If that is a clue to the structure of this Gospel we see that it divides naturally into three: (1) 1:1–4:16, *The person of Jesus the Messiah*; (2) 4:17–16:20, *The proclamation of Jesus the Messiah*; (3) 16:21–28:20, *The suffering, death and resurrection of Jesus the Messiah* (so J.D. Kingsbury).

The teaching of the Gospel

R.V.G. Tasker observed that the key-note of Matthew's Gospel is, 'Jesus has fulfilled Jewish prophecy'; i.e. in Jesus the Old Testament revelation is brought to its destined conclusion and realisation.

1. *The series of twelve citations from the Old Testament*, which Matthew sees as fulfilled in the life of Jesus, make this insight explicit (see 1:23; 2:6, 15, 17, 23; 3:3; 4:14; 8:17; 12:17–21; 13:35; 21:4; 27:9). These quotations are not all predictions of the Messiah's life, fulfilled in the actions of Jesus, but they include elements of a typology which is seen as fundamental to understanding the Gospel. For example, the quotation in 2:15, 'Out of Egypt have I called my son', is from Hosea 11:1 where 'son' denotes Israel, the people of God, as it does in Exodus 4:22. It is important to Matthew because it relates to the fulfilment in the life of Jesus of the prophetic theme of redemption thought of as a second exodus under the 'second Redeemer' (the Jews called Moses 'the first Redeemer', and the Messiah 'the second Redeemer'). Accordingly, it is in Jesus the Son of God that the new Israel is comprehended; it is he who brings about redemption out of sin and death and into participation in the 'promised land' (the 'inheritance') of the kingdom of God. These New Testament testimonies, far from being arbitrary as some allege, form a profound interpretation of Jesus in relation to the purpose of God revealed in the Old Testament.

2. *The presentation of Jesus* in Matthew's Gospel is given a unique slant in the opening sentence of the book: Jesus is introduced as *the Christ* (the Messiah), the *son of David* and *son of Abraham*. The appeal to the Jew is immediately obvious. As Son of David Jesus is recognised as the King-Messiah. In the time of Jesus the Jews were also beginning to look upon the Messiah as *Son of God*, the King who is installed as Son of God to represent the Son of God, Israel. The narrative of the virgin birth of Jesus points to a deeper understanding of Jesus as the Son of God in terms of unique relation to the Father; the conception by the Spirit further points to the activity of Jesus as the Messiah who initiates the time of salvation, the kingdom of God, since the Spirit belongs essentially to the time of the kingdom of God. As Son of God and *Son of Man* Jesus fulfils the role of the *Servant of the Lord*; by his total service of God and man he brings the kingdom of salvation that is to be completed at the end of the times.

3. *The interpretation of the Law*, as of the rest of the scriptures, in the light of the ministry of Jesus, is of major importance to Matthew. For the Jew the scriptures meant above all the Law, of which the Prophets and the Writings were viewed as exposition. It is likely that the work of reformulating Judaism in terms of the Pharisaic understanding of the Law was already in process in Matthew's time and known to him (it took place in Jamnia and made Judaism a religion of the Law). Therefore the authoritative interpretation of the Law of God given by Jesus was of deepest significance. This is set out most clearly in the sermon on the mount, which is represented by Matthew as the counterpart of the Law promulgated through the first redeemer on Sinai. Here the Messiah elucidates the intent of the word of God declared to 'the men of old', i.e. Israel at Sinai, wholly in accord with the expectation of the Jews, that the Messiah would be occupied with the Law and would authoritatively teach it. Over against the exposition of the Pharisaic teachers of the Law gathered in extended conference at Jamnia, Matthew sets forth the divinely inspired exposition of the Law by the Messiah-Son of God.

4. *The church* is explicitly mentioned by Matthew alone among the evangelists, though the reality is fundamental to all of them. The basic tenet he sets forth is the recognition of the church as the people of the kingdom of God (16:17ff). These are the recipients of the new covenant (26:28), the new Israel to whom the newly enunciated 'Torah' (= Law) is delivered (21:43 and chs. 5–7). Matthew's condemnation of the nation Israel is frequently observed; it is certainly present (e.g. 11:20–24, 23:37–38, 27:25), but the sharpest criticism is levelled against Israel's teachers, the Pharisees (e.g. ch. 23). Matthew has not given up hope of Israel's conversion.

5. *The kingdom of God* is the supreme theme of Jesus's proclamation in Matthew; note especially 4:17, and 4:23 where the message of Jesus is described as 'the Gospel of the kingdom'. It is more apparent in Matthew than in the other Gospels that the promised kingdom of God is both initiated through the life and ministry of Jesus (e.g. 11:5,11,12; 12:28) and is to be consummated through his coming at the end of the age (e.g. ch. 25). Thus, Jesus the Messiah is the instrument of the kingdom of God in the totality of his work, on earth, in heaven, and from heaven.

The purpose of the Gospel
Matthew's intention is manifold, but a prime purpose is indicated by the intense concern manifest on the one hand for Israel (see 10:5,23) and on the other for the mission to the nations (see, above all, 28:18–20). No other Gospel comprehends so starkly this dual concern of the Lord for both Israel and the nations. Jesus is presented as the Messiah sent to the ancient people of God, in order that the kingdom of God may be given to them and to the whole world. Matthew therefore writes that Jews and Gentiles hearing the Gospel may attain the prom-

ise of the kingdom of God and together rise to the destined vocation of God's people, that of being the servant-people under the Servant-Messiah to bring light to all nations, so fulfilling the lofty vision of Isaiah 40–55. Such is the function of the church, to which the completion of the revelation of God in Christ is imparted, along with the call to realise that 'better righteousness' which Christ embodied and makes possible (5:20; 11:28–30).

To explain to Jew and Gentile the significance of Jesus, Son of God, Saviour and Lord of the kingdom, is Matthew's supreme purpose.

Palestine in the time of Jesus

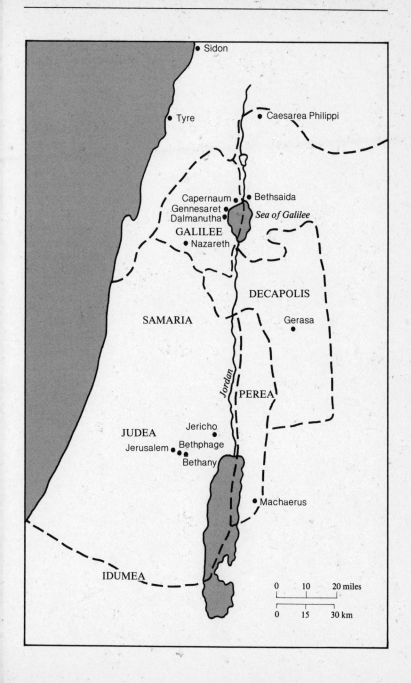

Sidon

Tyre

Caesarea Philippi

Capernaum
Gennesaret
Dalmanutha
Bethsaida
Sea of Galilee
GALILEE
Nazareth

DECAPOLIS

SAMARIA

Gerasa

Jordan

PEREA

Jericho

JUDEA
Jerusalem
Bethphage
Bethany

Machaerus

IDUMEA

| 0 | 10 | 20 miles |
| 0 | 15 | 30 km |

Matthew: Contents

1:1–17 The genealogy of Jesus

The opening phrase of Matthew's Gospel, 'The book of the *genesis* of Jesus Christ', alludes to two well known passages of the Old Testament: Genesis 2:4 and 5:1. In the Greek Old Testament the latter reads, 'The book of the *genesis* of Adam', and the former, 'The book of the *genesis* of the heavens and earth'; in both cases the term 'genesis' signifies origin, rather than simply genealogy or birth. Genesis 2:4–4:26 introduces the significant beginnings of the story of man; Matthew may well intend the phrase to introduce not only the genealogy of Jesus, but the significant beginnings of Jesus prior to his ministry.

Observe that Jesus is called 'son of David' before 'son of Abraham'; this opening sentence of the Gospel is evidently penned with the conscious intention of presenting a genealogy of Jesus through the royal line. It begins with Abraham, the father of the Jews to whom the promise of a divine inheritance was made, and ends up with the royal Messiah through whom the promise is actualised.

The inclusion of women in the genealogy is often commented on. They had three features in common: (i) they were aliens, or linked with such (Tamar and Rahab were Canaanites, Ruth a Moabitess, Bathsheba the wife of Uriah the Hittite), which is consonant with the Messiah sprung from them as the Saviour of the nations as well as of the Jews; (ii) there is something irregular with their unions with their partners, yet they made possible the continued line of the Messiah; (iii) they played an important role in God's plan, and so were seen by the Jews as notable instruments of the Spirit.

Matthew's emphasis on three sets of *fourteen* generations (17) has provoked many suggestions. The letters of David's name in Hebrew add up to fourteen (letters were used for numbers in Hebrew) – the genealogy could be a kind of acrostic on the name David. Fourteen as a multiple of seven was a significant number to Jews – they reckoned fourteen high priests from Aaron to Solomon's temple, and fourteen from Solomon till Jaddua, the last high priest mentioned in the Old Testament. Did Matthew reflect that Jesus was born after six lots of seven generations from Abraham, i.e. six weeks of generations, leading to the seventh week, the fullness of time? Certainly the genealogy reminds us that the hand of the Lord was on Israel's history, preparing for the birth of the Messiah.

TO THINK ABOUT: Is the hand of God as powerful in the affairs of history between the coming of the Son of God to initiate the kingdom of salvation and his coming in glory to consummate it? Is it seen as clearly in your affairs and mine?

1:18–25 The birth of Jesus

The circumstances of the revelation to Mary of her election to give birth to the Messiah are not mentioned by Matthew. The barest facts alone are related: Mary was betrothed to Joseph, but before the marriage process could be completed she was 'found to be with child of the Holy Spirit'. But that is the all-important fact. The point of emphasis is not the birth *of a virgin*, though that is plainly stated, but the birth *of the Spirit*, the mighty power of God at work in the world. The significance of this is complex.

1. The Old Testament anticipates that the Messiah would be equipped by the Holy Spirit for the accomplishment of his task (see, for example, Isa. 42:1). From his conception onwards, Jesus is the object of the Spirit's operation, that he may be his perfect instrument for the revelation of God and achievement of his redemptive purpose. Every word and deed of Jesus in his ministry bears this out. The Lord and the Spirit are inseparable (2 Cor. 3:17).

2. Since the Spirit is the agent of new creation, the conception of Jesus by the Spirit intimates the beginning of that work which will issue in new life for the world. While the baptism of Jesus, with its accompanying descent of the Spirit, marks the beginning of his public ministry, the whole enterprise was possible only because it was the fruit of a life from God and in God. The new creation began in Bethlehem, was manifest in the deeds of Jesus's ministry, erupted in power at Easter, and will blaze forth in glory at the coming of the Lord.

3. The emphasis on birth by the Spirit disallows the popular view that the birth from a virgin was the necessary *means* of the Incarnation of the Son of God. It was less a *means* than a *sign*, which was what v. 23 denoted in the prophetic utterance of Isaiah 7:14. As Barth once said, the virgin birth was not a condition but an accompanying miracle of the Incarnation, pointing to the great deed of God.

Isaiah 7:14 was given a greater fulfilment by the Spirit's action than the prophet could have foreseen (that's not unusual for the divine action!). The sign to King Ahaz of the birth from a girl of a child, whose name Immanuel indicates that God is with Judah to judge and deliver them, is eclipsed by the sign of the birth from a virgin of one *in* whom God is present with his people; he is present for judgement and for a deliverance which will issue in life from the dead.

TO THINK ABOUT: Jesus is what he signifies: the salvation of God ('Jesus'!) and the presence of God ('Immanuel'!). That is the heart of God's 'open secret', to be proclaimed to the ends of the earth: 'Christ *in* you, the hope of *glory*' (Col. 1:27).

2:1–12 Wise men from the East

The story of the 'Magi' (astrologer-priests) is one of the most remarkable incidents in the life of Jesus. We know from ancient records that such men in Babylonia and Parthia (= Armenia) were deeply interested in Palestine. Zoroastrianism had acquainted them with the hope of a saviour-king who should rule in a kingdom of God, and it was believed that he would arise in the west. The Magier-king, Tiridates of Parthia, actually journeyed to Rome in AD 66 to do homage to Nero, on the ground that the stars pointed to him as the awaited king of the world (a sad mis-reading!).

Note the following concerning the star of Jesus: (1) in 7 BC there was a conjunction of Jupiter (viewed as the god of the Romans) with Saturn (understood as the star of the Jews) in Pisces (the first of the Zodiac signs), something which happened once only in 257–8 years; this could have been interpreted as marking the coming rule of the Jews over Rome. (2) There was an ancient tradition that a star would appear two years before the birth of the Messiah. (3) Chinese astronomers noted the appearance of an evanescent star or comet in 5 BC and again in 4 BC – a phenomenon visible also in Palestine. (4) Jesus was born 5–4 BC, for Herod died in 4 BC. (5) The reference to *two years* in v. 16 suggests that the Magi had seen the earlier sign, concluded that the saviour-king was at hand, and journeyed to Palestine following the second 'star'.

Equally remarkable is the reaction of the Jewish leaders and Herod to the arrival of the Magi: they were 'troubled', and in Herod's heart was murder. Here is the first lesson Matthew would have us learn: God revealed the saviour-king to Gentiles, whose knowledge of God was clouded, while the people to whom he came were unready and unwelcoming; this was prophetic of the history to be unfolded in the life of Jesus and the mission of the church. Secondly, Jesus fulfilled not only the prophecies of the revealed word of God, but the religious hopes and aspirations of nations, which also sprang from divine revelation although imperfectly grasped. As Paul was later to say to the superstitious Lycaonians: God has not left himself without witness among the nations (Acts 14:17), a theme which he expounded more fully to the Athenians (Acts 17:22–31).

TO THINK ABOUT: The Magi offered special gifts to the infant Redeemer: gold, frankincense, myrrh – 'for a King, for a Man, and for God', commented Juvencus (or for King, for God, for Sacrifice', Origen). What offering can I bring to Christ that is special to *me?*

2:13–23 Egypt and Nazareth

Here are three paragraphs, each concluding with a citation from the Old Testament. The first tells of Joseph's departure to Egypt with Jesus and Mary to escape Herod's wrath, and of their remaining there till Herod's death; thereby a fulfilment of the prophetic word was made possible: 'Out of Egypt have I called my son'. The evangelist knew that Hosea 11:1 has in view God's adopted 'son' Israel, but he sees here the commencement of fulfilment of a chain of Old Testament prophecy, that God was to achieve another and greater exodus for his people and bring them into the promised land of his kingdom. Jesus therefore goes down into Egypt, as Israel did before him.

Herod's attempt to kill the infant King by murdering the infants judged to be his age is in keeping with Herod's behaviour in his latter years when he suffered from arterial sclerosis and was subject to murderous outbursts. To Matthew two things are significant here. The 'second Redeemer' (the Messiah) was subject to the endeavour of a tyrant to kill him, as the 'first redeemer' (Moses) had been. Verse 20 takes up the language of Exodus 4:19, where Moses is told to return to his people since 'all the men who were seeking your life are dead'. Further, the lament of the mothers in Bethlehem echoes that of 'Rachel', the archetypal mother of Israel, as she wept for her children sent into captivity (Jer. 31:15); but the prophecy is in reality a consolation: 'Rachel' may weep now, but she is told to cease from tears, for 'there is hope for your future' – deliverance is at hand and the children will return (Jer. 31:16,17).

Joseph's taking Jesus to Galilee, to avoid the irascible Archelaus of Judea, fulfils what was spoken by the prophets, 'He shall be called a *Nazarene*'. Matthew will have had various prophetic passages in mind here (NB. *prophets*, v. 23, is in the plural, not singular as elsewhere). 'Nazarene' denoted a man from Nazareth and, since Nazareth was despised, the term could be used contemptuously (see, for example, John 1:46, Isa. 53:3). The root of 'Nazarene' in Hebrew was virtually identical with *netser*, the 'branch', a figure for the Messiah in Isaiah 11:1; it is also related to the term 'preserved' (*netsire*) in Isaiah 49:6, suggesting that Jesus was the Preserver who would restore Israel and save the nations. Even closer is the Hebrew term for *Nazarite*; conceivably there's an echo here of Samson as a type of the Messiah.

TO THINK ABOUT: Our uncertainty about this does not put us at a disadvantage. God, in and through Jesus, chooses many different ways to show his solidarity with his people in their distresses and to illustrate the salvation he provides for them. See, for example, Isaiah 63:7–12.

3:1–12 The ministry of John the Baptist

For the Jew 'in those days' (v. 1) the age of prophecy had long passed away; there were sages and seers, but the restoration of prophecy belonged to the end time (see 1 Maccabees 4:44–46: the altar stones in the temple, defiled by pagan blasphemies, were set aside 'until a prophet should arise who could be consulted about them'). John claimed to be neither the prophet of Deuteronomy 18:15, nor Elijah; but he and the people recognised that his ministry of preparing the Lord's way signified the renewal of prophecy in the last times, immediately prior to the kingdom of God.

Strikingly, John's preaching is summarised in v. 2 in the same language as that of Jesus in 4:17. But there is a difference, pointed out by Matthew's Old Testament citations: in John's preaching the 'nearness' of the kingdom was a promise (v. 3: '*Prepare* the way of the Lord'); for Jesus the nearness of the kingdom was present (4:16, for 'the people who sat in darkness . . . *light has dawned*'). John bridged Old Testament prophecy and the appearance of the Messiah; Jesus introduced the kingdom.

As to the terms of their preaching, note that kingdom *of heaven* means the same as kingdom *of God*; 'heaven' is a reverential synonym for God (see Dan. 4:25–26); to 'repent' meant to *turn* from sin to God, not simply being sorry for sins (compare Ezek. 33:10–11).

The Qumran priests applied the text of v. 3 to themselves, reading it, '*In the wilderness* prepare the way of the Lord' so settled in the wilderness area where John ministered. Their daily baptisms with repentance for sins, which replaced the sacrifices of the (to them) corrupt temple, are the closest parallel we know to John's baptism. But while they baptised daily and prepared for the Messiah by studying the Law in cloisters, John went out and pleaded with people to be ready for the Messiah by turning to God and being once for all baptised.

The stern message to the Jewish leaders (vs. 7–10) is that they should show genuine repentance, and not trust to Abraham's merits; for the coming Messiah will exercise a powerful judgement which will include God's people (v. 12); his 'baptism' will be not with water but with the mighty Spirit of God and fire, by which he will destroy the wicked and cleanse the righteous and give them life for the age to come (v. 11 is an echo of Isa. 4:2–5 and similar prophetic sayings).

TO THINK ABOUT: 'When we have heartily repented of wrong we should let all the waves of forgetfulness roll over it, and go forward unburdened to meet the future' (H. W. Beecher).

3:13–17 The baptism of Jesus

'Jesus came from Galilee to the Jordan to be baptized by him' (13). Why? John baptized 'for repentance' in view of the Messiah's baptism in Spirit and fire (11); how could the Messiah submit to a baptism for sinners in preparation for his own judgement? Christians have puzzled over that question from earliest times, and Matthew helps us understand the conundrum.

One thing is evident from the Gospels: Jesus did not come *as a sinner* needing John's baptism. Nor is it conceivable that he had no idea who he was, nor that John was totally ignorant. On this Adolf Schlatter affirmed: 'The belief that Jesus went to his baptism without any ideas and then, taken aback by the sign, returned home as the Messiah, was as impossible for Matthew as the notion of a baptism performed without any exchange of words'. John would not have baptized Jesus, or anyone else, without questions; verses 14–15 are our only hint in the Gospels of the nature of that conversation. It led John to the utterance of v. 14: 'I need your baptism, and you are coming to receive mine?' The reply of v. 15 is an imperative; not, 'That may be true, but never mind . . .', rather, 'Let it be so – *at once!*' It is necessary for Jesus to carry out in action 'all righteousness', i.e. all that God would have him do to bring about the salvation of the kingdom of God. Jesus therefore in his baptism does two inseparable things: he identifies himself with the sinful people he came to save and he consecrates himself to God for the task of saving them.

The result of the baptism is the opening of the heavens, the descent of the Spirit on Jesus, and the Father's words, 'This is my beloved son, with whom I am well pleased.' That is more than a simple indication of God's pleasure at the event; it is a sign that the Lord of Hosts has now embarked on the accomplishment of his purpose through his anointed one. Heaven is being opened to man, the Spirit of the kingdom comes on the anointed one for his task of bringing it, and Jesus is declared to be the royal son (Ps. 2:7) who is fulfilling the vocation of the servant of the Lord (Isa. 42:1). *The kingdom of God is on its way!*

TO THINK ABOUT: The baptism of Jesus was as unique as the ministry it initiated – as unique as his sacrifice on the cross and his resurrection as Lord of the kingdom. Yet he calls his followers to be one with him in the kingdom work, as he became one with us for the kingdom. Has our baptism been followed by a like consecration to the service of God and those for whom heaven was opened?

4:1–11 The temptations of Jesus

Scholars have differed in their understanding of this passage. Does it present Jesus as the representative of a new Israel overcoming the devil's temptations in the wilderness for forty days, over against Israel's failure in its forty years in the desert? Or does it contrast Jesus with Adam, who succumbed to the devil's temptation and brought ruin on mankind? Or does it portray the Messiah, fresh from his dedication in baptism, tempted to do God's work in the devil's ways? Reflection suggests that all three approaches are necessary and interdependent.

Jesus was sent as God's Messiah for Israel, through whose victory the nation should fulfil its destined role in the world (it is not without significance that Jesus's answers to the temptations are all from Deuteronomy, 8:3; 6:16; 6:13, which is addressed to Israel in the wilderness). But Jesus was the Messiah for the whole world; as the second Adam he was called to achieve the obedience which all have failed to give, an obedience which was to end death for all mankind. And because Jesus was baptised *as* Messiah, he is led by the Spirit to contest the field with the Tempter; for the kingdom of God comes precisely through overcoming the rule of the devil and the power of sin (see John 12:31–32).

TO THINK ABOUT: The temptations of Jesus were less an argument than a struggle, from which Jesus emerged victorious. As always he proved to be stronger than the 'strong one' (of Matthew 12:29) through his dependence on God and God's 'whole armour' (compare Isa. 49:24, 25; 59:16–19). Through such reliance we also may know victory – for ourselves and for others.

Questions for further study and discussion on Matthew 1:1–4:11

1. Does 'the virgin birth' divide Jesus from or bind him to humanity (cf. John 1:13)?

2. What counterparts are there to the Magi today?

3. Who else might have been anxious to kill the child Jesus (2:20)?

4. Consider the glory and limitations of John's ministry (see also, Matt. 11:2–11; John 3:27–30).

5. Why do you think Jesus told his disciples of his temptations? (For one answer see Dostoevsky's 'Grand Inquisitor' in *The Brothers Karamazov*).

4:12–25 The beginning of the Galilean ministry

Matthew supplies three paragraphs which serve as summary introductions to his account of the ministry of Jesus which follows. His statement, 'Jesus *withdrew* into Galilee', is intriguing. We know from the Gospel of John that Jesus had already ministered in Judea, concurrently with John the Baptist; for Matthew the departure to Galilee may signify the withdrawal from the area where John's ministry had been resisted to another which must hear the word of God (compare 2:22; 12:15; 15:21).

The citing of Isaiah 9:1–2 in vs. 12–16 is important not only because it shows that scripture located Jesus's ministry in Galilee, but because it illustrates the significance of that ministry for the people of Galilee. The gloom and anguish which was theirs is now being scattered by the shining of a great light. In the Bible 'light' is a synonym for salvation; with Jesus the salvation of the promised kingdom of God had arrived. This is the burden of the proclamation summarised in v. 17: 'The kingdom of heaven has drawn near'. Its powers and blessings are available through the Proclaimer.

The account of the calling of the earliest disciples is integral to a Gospel narrative; for, apart from the historical importance of knowing how Peter and his friends became followers of Jesus, it is necessary to know that following Jesus has always meant being involved in the ministry of the kingdom.

Verses 23–25 summarise the ministry of Jesus under three heads: *teaching* in synagogues, which especially relates to exposition of the scriptures (cf. the account of Jesus in Nazareth, Luke 4:16–21); *preaching* to all and sundry on the other six days of the week the good news of the kingdom of God; and *healing* people afflicted with all sorts of diseases – a manifestation of the kingdom of God in action. The main theme of the preaching has already been stated in v. 17. The teaching of Jesus is about to be given its classic statement in the sermon on the mount (chs. 5–7), and the ministry of healing will be exemplified in chs. 8–9 which immediately follow the sermon.

TO THINK ABOUT: 'Jesus's disciples were not simply *auditors* (as at Qumran and in the Rabbinic schools); they were collaborators as "fishers of men" ' (David Hill). How well am I collaborating with Jesus?

5:1–12 The beatitudes

The sermon on the mount has long been recognised as the digest of a sermon of Jesus, amplified by excerpts from sermons preached on other occasions – A. M. Hunter spoke of twenty possible such sermons (his little book, *Design for Life*, is an excellent guide to the meaning of these chapters). The further suggestion has been made that Matthew has given us the teaching of Jesus drawn up for Jewish converts, and Luke the teaching for Gentile converts; that is worth considering, and it has an important corollary: the sermon is not primarily the good news of the kingdom, but the life characteristic of those in the kingdom. The statement of Ghandi: 'The message of Jesus is contained in the sermon on the mount, unadulterated and taken as a whole', laudable as it is, is incorrect; the message of Jesus is that the kingdom of God has come to men in his words and action, which culminated in the cross and resurrection; the sermon therefore is for those who have received the word of the kingdom and know its salvation.

The sermon opens with a number of beatitudes, which have been described as 'blessings in the form of teaching'. The term 'blessed', better 'happy' (Greek *makarios*), is a rendering of the Hebrew interjection, 'Oh the happiness of . . .' (see, for example, Ps. 1:1; 32:1). The people whose happiness is so emphatically declared are described in the first half of each beatitude and the ground of their happiness is stated in the second half of each. Fundamentally the people so described are not models of saintly achievement, but people who have nothing and know they are nothing but look to God for his salvation (for an indication of who the poor, meek etc. are, see Ps. 37). To such as are in that position the promise is given that they shall have everything – everything, that is, that God can give man in his kingdom of glory – for the second half of each beatitude describes the blessings of the 'kingdom of heaven'. Together the halves constitute a notable description of the meaning of the kingdom of God for believers. Characteristically, then, the sermon begins with the bases of the gospel and indirectly suggests that those who have nothing and are nothing should imitate their Father in his grace (7–9).

TO THINK ABOUT: The beatitude of verses 11, 12 probably belongs to the time when to be associated with Jesus entailed the hostility directed to him. Consider the implications of v. 11, 'Oh the *happiness* you have when you are reproached . . .!', and v. 12, rendered in Luke 6:23, 'Rejoice, and *leap in the dance* . . .!' Why is this sentiment so foreign to us today?

5:13–20 Salt, light and scripture

'You are the salt of the earth.' For what purpose? For taste, yes, but still more (in a hot climate) to prevent corruption. But the question follows: 'If salt becomes tasteless, how shall it be made salty?' We know from Jewish writings that some Jews objected to this saying of Jesus; for salt does not, in fact, lose its taste. That is so if it is *pure*; but the salt bought by Jesus's hearers was rock salt or taken from the Dead Sea shores, mixed with grit and sand. Salt can be rendered useless by dirt, and is then thrown out to mix with the dust and dirt of the street.

'You are the light of the world.' Note that Jesus does not say, 'You *ought* to be the light . . .' but 'You *are* . . .' This they become who receive his word and follow him, for then they belong to him who is the Light of the world (John 8:12); when his word abides in them the light of God shines through them. They don't have to struggle to be light; it is as obvious as the twinkling lights of a town on the hilltop (14). They simply have to ensure that they don't put the light out; for the most common way of extinguishing a light in Jewish households was to place a bucket over it – to prevent air from getting to the wick and stop sparks from flying. No one lights a lamp in order immediately to put it out. As lamps are lit to shine on a stand, so disciples are made to shine in the world by their Christlike deeds (16).

The paragraph on the law and true righteousness (17–20) sets out to correct the slander that Jesus had come to abolish the law. The Pharisees argued, on the basis of their understanding of the law, that he did precisely this. On the contrary, Jesus came to fulfil the law and the prophecies and that not simply by teaching but by deeds that enacted their demand and promise. The law of which 18–19 speaks is likely to refer to God's demand for righteousness, not the prescriptions of the ceremonial law (compare Matt. 15:10–20). As the Lord came to fulfil both law and prophets in his actions, thereby opening the kingdom to all, so his followers must live in the righteousness of God in order to inherit it (20, compare 6:33).

TO THINK ABOUT: Compare v. 18 with 24:35. The law is for this age. When the new creation comes the word of Jesus stands, for it passes into an eternal fulfilment in the kingdom that knows no end.

5:21–26 Murder and its relations

One designation of the sermon on the mount is 'the law of the Messiah', and this aspect is especially apparent in 5:21–48. Declarations from the law given to 'the men of old', i.e. the generation around the time of Sinai, are cited, sometimes the with interpretation currently held, and Jesus authoritatively declares God's real intention in the law. The whole passage exemplifies how the Lord, in the spirit of 5:17, would have the principles of the Old Testament law embodied in the higher righteousness of the kingdom.

The statement in 21–22 following the Old Testament command not to kill is paraphrased by A. H. McNeile: 'The Rabbis say that murder is liable to judgement, but I say that anger, its equivalent, is liable to (divine) judgement. And (the Rabbis say that) abusive language such as *raka* ('sheepshead!') is punishable by the local court, but I say that abusive language such as *more* ('fool!'), its equivalent, is punishable by the fire of Gehenna.' Here Jesus draws attention to the gravity of the anger and hate which lie at the root of murder, *both* being offensive to God. Jesus similarly cuts across the tidy, Pharisaic, distinctions between insults for which one may be taken to court and those which one can get away with; any language which makes a man contemptible before his fellows is remembered before God – against the accuser. 'Soul murder' is a sin against God as well as against man.

This principle is brought home in the sphere of worship. If someone is holding a grudge against another, it is because he thinks that the other has wronged him, and the responsibility to put the matter right rests with the other ('with *you*', said Jesus!). In such circumstances to offer a sacrifice – or any other kind of worship – is useless to God; one must first get reconciled with the brother, then God will listen to prayer and receive an offering.

That leads to a parable of judgement. The apparently worldly-wise advice of 25–26 is a thinly veiled exhortation to be reconciled to God, against whom we have offended, lest we be condemned with a judgement from which there is no escape (the context of Luke's equivalent, Luke 12:58–9, makes this plain).

TO THINK ABOUT: It is crystal clear from our passage that expressions of love to God are valueless without love to people, whether they are fellow-Christians, neighbours or strangers. It is possible to profess the former and find that God is against us. If the Lord would have us apply 23–24 or 25–26 to ourselves, we would be wise to act accordingly, *quickly!* (25)

5:27–37 Holiness in life and language

Verses 27–28 extend the application of the law against adultery exactly as 21–24 extend the significance of the prohibition against murder: God is concerned with the heart, not simply with external acts. (For an example of v. 28 note David's relation with Bathsheba; the mischief was done in David's contemplation of her, before the adultery was performed and the murder of her husband carried out.)

Strong language is used in 29–30 to indicate the necessity for renunciation of everything that would lead us into sin. The right hand and right eye are most important; but if even *they* tempt you to sin, said Jesus, cut them out and throw them away! Literally so? No, for every man's right eye and right hand would then have been on the ground before Jesus – a shocking mess! He was calling for the whole body, the whole person, to be consecrated to God, and anything which keeps us from him to be renounced.

In harmony with the above Jesus insists that a man treat his wife according to God's will (the motives are elaborated in Matt. 19:3–9). The prescription cited from Deuteronomy 24:1–4 was not given to initiate divorce but to regulate contemporary practices; in our Lord's time it was abused, making frequent divorce possible and resulting in successive relations with women. Since women had no recourse in that society but to remarry they, too, were involved in the compromised situation. Jesus reaffirmed the divine intention of life-long marriage.

Again, in 33–37, Jesus goes behind the Old Testament regulations concerning oaths (Lev. 19:12; Num. 30:2; Deut. 23:21), which were for the purpose of making people keep their word solemnly pledged before the Lord, and sweeps aside oaths altogether. He does this partly because they appeal to things which really stand for God (as in 34,35), and over which we have no control (as in 36), and partly because they are needless. A simple Yes, or No, is sufficient for one whose word is trustworthy. Anything beyond this, said Jesus, comes from 'the evil' (one, or nature of man). But the Old Testament gives regulations concerning oaths! Apparently Jesus sees the misuse of oaths as comparable to the devil's misuse of the word of God, as he had experienced it in the wilderness temptations.

TO THINK ABOUT: God and truth are inseparable. To love God is to love truth. Lips that praise the Lord should speak truth as God does.

5:38–48 Love and revenge

Earlier Jesus spoke of those whom we are in a position to wrong. Here he has in view those who are in a position to wrong us.

Observe that the injunction of Exodus 21:24 and Deuteronomy 19:21 does not *invent* a law of revenge but *tempers* an existing institution with justice. To lose one tooth is no justification for knocking out a mouthful of one's enemy – no more than one is permitted! The principle is intended to stop the fearful law of the vendetta which has no end. Jesus again takes the Old Testament principle to a limit beyond its horizon: take no revenge, instead show love. He cites three typical situations from life: first, a case of personal insult (39: a slap on the right cheek is a back-hander); second, a suit at law (40: a creditor cannot take the outer cloak, which is used as a blanket, but he can take the tunic); third, a demand for forced labour (41: probably from a soldier who demands a man's donkey to carry his burden; if it is given, the animal is not seen again, so the owner has to go with it). These illustrations go beyond passive resistance; to offer the other cheek, to let a man have the coat which he cannot take by law, to offer to go another mile with a representative of an oppressive power, are expressions of a love more powerful than the injustice which seeks to crush.

The final injunction of v. 44 is in exactly the same spirit. Jews have sometimes asked, with regard to this saying, 'Where in the Talmud does it say that the Jew must love his neighbour and hate his enemy?' The answer is, 'Nowhere'. But the Talmud largely reflects Judaism after Jesus. Even early Judaism set the application of Leviticus 19:18 firmly in its context: there 'neighbour' = fellow-Jew; the Jew has no such obligation to the Gentiles. But the most enthusiastic Jews of the time of Jesus taught just what Jesus said one should not. The Qumran Essenes wrote that a man must 'walk perfectly before him (God) according to all things which have been revealed . . . He shall love each one of the sons of light according to his lot in the council of God, and hate each one of the sons of darkness according to his guilt at the time of God's vengeance' (D.S.D. 1, 7ff). Jesus, on the contrary, calls on God's people to be 'perfect, as your heavenly Father is perfect' (48); not, of course, in the perfection of his glorious holiness, which is unthinkable, but *in the generosity of grace* (see the parallel in Luke 6:36).

TO THINK ABOUT: The joy that exceeds (12), and the righteousness that exceeds (20), culminate in a love that exceeds (46, 47). A glorious crescendo!

6:1–8 Righteousness, on and off stage

The devotional life of Jews in the time of Jesus found expression in three directions: in almsgiving, prayer and fasting. These are dealt with in 1–4, 5–8, 16–18, with the model prayer added in 9–13. Jesus shows that they are all acceptable to God, providing they are not spoiled by being directed to man instead of God. When this happens the godly become 'hypocrites', i.e. play-actors; they act religiously on a stage for people to see and are paid for their trouble, but not by God.

The expression in v. 1, 'practising your piety' (literally *righteousness*) reflects contemporary usage: righteousness was expressed supremely in almsgiving. The thought is illustrated in Tobit 12:8–9: 'It is better to give alms than to lay up gold; alms delivers from death, and it shall purge away all sin'. Such an attitude is far from Jesus, but the importance to him of giving to the poor is plain (compare, for example, Matt. 25:31–46).

The comment on prayer in 5–8 again reflects Jewish habits. The law regulated prayer, as it did everything else. Three times were prescribed for prayer: morning and afternoon, when sacrifices were offered in the temple, and an extra one in the evening. Curiously, some Pharisees always happened to be at street corners or chief squares at these set times for prayer! Jesus states that a store room (or inner room) is a more fit place for communion with God. He also refers to pagan prayer habits. The latter had an expression *fatigare deos* – 'to make the god weary', till their resistance was worn out and they gave way to the petitioners. All such notions are far from one who knows God as Father. He knows our hearts and in his love is ready to help us at all times.

TO THINK ABOUT: Karl Heim's comment on v. 6: 'We should so talk to God, as if we have already died and had the earth behind us, and had nothing else than our soul, and this were with God entirely alone'. Such prayer revolutionises life.

Questions for further study and discussion on Matthew 4:12–6:8

1. 'It would be a great point gained if people would only consider that it was a sermon, and was preached, not an act that was passed' (James Denney). Consider 5:21–48 in the light of this comment on the sermon on the mount.

2. How does Jesus's preaching of the gospel relate to the Christian message today?

3. Should we expect people in our society to live according to the beatitudes? Why, or why not?

4. How can the principles of 5:38–42 be practised in a nuclear age?

5. If God knows what we need before we ask (6:8), why pray?

6. What sort of treatment in our society might correspond to the 'persecution' mentioned in 5:44, and what would be our appropriate response?

7. What is the principle behind the command not to swear oaths (5:33–37) and how does it apply to us today?

8. What impositions on your time, energy or money do you find irritating? In the light of 5:41,42, is there any other way in which you can regard these situations?

6:9–18 The disciple's prayer

It is a striking fact that when the prayer taught by Jesus is put back into his own language, both in Matthew's and Luke's versions, it has rhythm and rhyme. Jewish poetry did not rhyme, apart from a notable exception – the prayer said by Jews three times daily (the Eighteen Benedictions). So it seems likely that Jesus intended the prayer he taught to be regarded as a model for prayer and to be remembered in order to use it when praying.

The Jewish daily prayer originally had twelve long petitions, six for the people and six for the kingdom of God – in that order. Jesus gave six short petitions, three for the kingdom and three for ourselves – in that order. This accords with his teaching and his whole life (compare Matt. 6:33).

In Luke 11:2 the prayer begins simply, 'Father', i.e. *Abba*; the 'our' in Matthew is evidently for congregational use. No Jew ever addressed God as *Abba*; it was an infant's word when talking to his 'daddy', and was considered unworthy of God. The disciples never got over their astonishment at this teaching of Jesus; that's why they taught the name 'Abba' in every language in which the gospel went (compare Mark 14:36; Rom. 8:15; Gal. 4:6). The three petitions for the kingdom are in parallelism: 'Hallowed be thy name/Thy kingdom come/Thy will be done', and the phrase, 'as in heaven, so on earth', covers all three. The three petitions are for the manifestation of God's glory in the consummation of the kingdom brought by Christ.

The prayer for bread *for the coming day* (rather than 'daily' – to be prayed in the morning?) is placed before prayer for forgiveness. That's remarkable! It relates to real bread, not spiritual bread; it is a prayer for people who knew hunger. Verse 13 is best read, 'Do not allow us to be led into temptation', i.e. to succumb to it; the Lord of all powers can give us victory over the evil one. The final benediction is not in the earliest manuscripts; it may have been used by Jesus on various occasions and added later by his disciples.

The paragraph on fasting is in the same spirit as 1–4, 5–8. Jesus did not normally fast, nor ask his disciples to do so (see Mark 2:18–20). Here he addresses those who do fast, and speaks of it as an offering to God which must be made on similar conditions as charitable giving and prayer.

TO THINK ABOUT: Only God can enable us to render a genuine devotional life to him and maintain us in holy and happy relations with him; compare Romans 8:26, 27.

6:19–34 Faith at the crossroads

The binding theme of our passage is the relation of faith and the business of living in a world where money appears to be a necessity for survival.

Some set their hearts on treasure on earth, investing (as frequently in the east) in silks and satins and precious metals; nature has a way of dealing with these things, and thieves finish off the job (19). Treasure 'in heaven' is with God; since his kingdom is for eternity, the treasure is equally lasting.

The parable of 22–23 adapts Proverbs 20:27, using 'eye' instead of 'spirit', so producing a picture which, in this context, suggests that to have a diseased eye spiritually is to have one's eye on material things, and so a covetous spirit; to have a healthy eye is to see straight and to have one's desires set on God, and that is to enjoy the true light of life.

The saying on the two masters (24) indicates that some try a compromise, seeking treasures on earth *and* in heaven. That entails a marriage of covetousness with godliness and it cannot be done. No man can serve two masters; he can give time to two *employers*, but he cannot be a slave to two *masters*, since both demand all. The alternative master here is 'mammon', which basically means what a person trusts in – an extraordinary name for money; it demands and secures the whole-hearted allegiance of its followers who worship and serve at its shrine. God won't have idolaters after money in his kingdom. Hesitant faith has to choose at this parting of ways.

Verses 25–34 are in a gentler strain, for they are directed to people who confess faith in God and await his kingdom but are constantly anxious and worried about everyday matters, as though faith and God's kingdom do not touch life's everyday affairs. Jesus bids such to recognise that our Father is creator and redeemer; his concern for his world is seen in his provision for the birds of the air and the beauty of the fields. He is concerned for our life in this world, just as he is concerned that we shall have his life in the world to come. Jesus therefore enunciates the maxim of v. 33. To seek God's kingdom is to ensure that we possess its blessings now and that we endeavour to serve it for God's glory, so that others may enter it and will stand with the king when he comes. That's enough for any day's work! Tomorrow can be left to God. For tomorrow God comes.

TO THINK ABOUT: 'Above all things do not touch Christianity unless you are willing to seek the kingdom of heaven first. I promise you a miserable existence if you seek it second' (Henry Drummond).

7:1–12 Judging and the golden rule

The opening statement of Jesus, taken out of context, could imply that no Christian should judge another person for any cause. On this basis many have deduced that a Christian may not be a magistrate. This kind of mistaken interpretation of the sermon is not infrequent. Jesus uttered many words of condemnation of hypocritical people, and Paul in 1 Corinthians 5:1–5 chastises a church for not judging a flagrant case of immorality. It is the attitude of *censoriousness* which is in mind, a condition which commonly denotes something wrong in the judgemental person ('When religious people begin backsliding, they begin backbiting!'). Verse 6 supplies a complement to 1–5: people who persistently ridicule the message of Christ should not have the holy things of God pressed on them. Jesus gave himself unstintingly to penitent sinners, but he had no word for the high priest (Mark 14:61), Herod (Luke 23:9) or, finally, Pilate (John 19:9).

The encouragement to prayer in 7–11 is applicable to all life's circumstances, but it receives a special application in its present context. It has been stated, 'The Sermon on the Mount gives no word as to the way of realising the perfection it preaches; it still remains a law'. On the contrary, Jesus never expected us to try to live in our own strength. Here he supplies the key: God's help is available to enable us to put into practice what Jesus declares. So *ask, seek, knock!*

Many have pointed out that the 'golden rule' (12) has been enunciated by other religious teachers though, curiously, almost always in a negative form ('Do *not* do to others what you do *not* wish to be done to yourself'). It is typical of Jesus to summarise God's law in a positive way. In reality it is a practical statement as to how the second part of the 'dual command' (Mark 12:29–31) may be put into effect. If it is placed in relation to the sermon its application is raised enormously: 'This verse means that we are to treat those socially and economically below us, those who are contemptuous toward us in smiting our cheeks, and those who are our enemies, as we would like to be treated were we in their place' (Stanley Jones). Such a view gives a content to the saying which judgemental advocates of the negative view could not have in mind. It entails a new approach to life – under the kingdom of the God who is love.

A PRAYER: Lord, help me to live by this rule today – and every day.

7:13–29 A call for self-examination

'The golden rule' forms the climax of the instruction in the sermon. Now follow warnings to 'examine yourselves and see whether you are in the faith', to use Paul's words. There are no fresh principles of action, but an underlining of the appeal of the sermon is given in order to drive home its message.

The figure of **the two ways** (13–14) is found in the Old Testament (Ps. 1; Jer. 21:8; Prov. 14:12). Jesus uses it to distinguish between the ways of man and the way of God; the former lead to 'destruction' (separation from God), the latter to 'life' (in the kingdom of God). Why a *narrow* gate and *narrow* way? Perhaps an indication that the gate is entered singly as we come in repentance to God, and the life is continued in constant renunciation of self. Those who find it are few, for even God's people were rejecting the word of the kingdom; but the Lord was advancing to a cross and resurrection so that the gates of the kingdom would be opened to all mankind. For an instructive parallel, see Matthew 8:11–12.

The simile of **the two trees** (15–20) is applied here to false teachers, whereas in Luke 6:43–45 it is applied generally. Its application to the former is due to the sad fact that wherever true prophecy arises, the possibility of false prophecy is present. 'By their fruits' the reality of their profession of faith and of their ministry in the Lord's name is known. Servants of God have to listen to these words carefully; Paul conveys a similar lesson in 1 Corinthians 3:10–15 (also addressed to leaders in the church).

The picture of **the two houses** assumes the Galilean hills, not the seaside. On hill slopes in dry seasons the foundation of a house may appear of little consequence but later on the rain storms fill dry river beds and make new channels, so that a poorly founded house could be swept down the slopes. Jesus does not have in mind the storms of life which test us, but the last trial we face before the throne of God. Then it will be revealed whether we have built on the sand of man's inadequate notions or on the rock of God's revelation in Christ.

TO THINK ABOUT: The sermon on the mount begins with gospel beatitudes and ends with searching the heart: 'Blessed are the poor . . . who build on the rock!' It is essential that we know where our foundations are, and that we continue to build our life according to the word of the Lord.

8:1–13 Authority to heal

Judged from any viewpoint, the first of the healings recorded by Matthew are remarkable, but to him they will have been deeply significant. They reveal that the word of Jesus was manifested not only in unparalleled teaching but also in unparalleled healing. And they reveal a unique attitude to the law.

Leprosy was a disease to be feared, not simply from the physical viewpoint, but because (in Jewish eyes) it was a defilement that separated the sufferer from both man and God. Hence the plea of the leper that Jesus should *cleanse* him (2). In touching the man Jesus showed disregard for physical danger and ceremonial pollution; yet he told the man to go to the priest to secure proof that he was healed and could mix again with people, as the law required (Lev. 14). This was an evidence of Jesus's conformity to the Mosaic law.

The healing of the centurion's 'boy' (the Greek term *pais* can mean child or servant) was equally remarkable. The centurion was probably an Arab, a Gentile (John describes him as a 'king's officer', i.e. in the service of Herod Antipas, John 4:46). Recent scholarship is inclined to believe that v. 7 should be read as a question: Jesus asks, 'Am *I* (emphatic) to come and heal him?' The centurion, living among Jews, knows that Jews do not enter Gentile houses lest they be defiled; he fully understands the query. No, he is not a fit person for Jesus to come into his house, but neither is it necessary – 'Only say the word . . .' This plea is based on a simple analogy: he, the centurion, bears the authority of his superiors, so that he has but to speak a word to his inferiors and they obey; similarly, it is inferred, Jesus bears authority bestowed by God, he has but to speak a word and his boy will be healed. Jesus 'marveled' at so spontaneous an expression of faith, and contrasted it with the faith he sought in Israel but did not find. The saying of vs. 10–12 primarily reflects Isaiah 25:6–9. Jesus declares that multitudes will stream from the ends of the earth and join the patriarchs in the kingdom feast, while the 'sons of the kingdom', its proper heirs, will be excluded from it. That will have been an unbelievable statement for Jews listening to Jesus: *they* cast out, and Gentiles, who should submit to them in the kingdom, *sitting down* with Abraham, Isaac and Jacob! It was meant to shock. The word of God must sometimes cut deep before it can heal.

TO THINK ABOUT: The path that leads from outer darkness into the banqueting hall is straightforward: it is faith that applies to itself the authoritative word of Jesus.

8:14–22 Works of the Son of man

As is characteristic of Matthew, his account of the healing of Peter's mother-in-law is compressed (he has much to include in his Gospel!). Mark recounts that it was when Jesus and his disciples left the synagogue and entered Peter's house that they told him of the illness of Peter's mother-in-law. Jesus at once went to her and touched her hand – something Jewish teachers avoided doing (a later rabbi explicitly stated: Only those sick people should be visited whose fever has gone). At the touch of Jesus the fever went! She instantly 'rose and served him'; Jesus's touch was intended to be noted, and emulated. Matthew's mention that other afflicted persons were brought to Jesus 'that evening' recalls Mark's note that it took place on the evening that closed the sabbath; the people did not wish to break the law. In the healing deeds of Jesus, Matthew sees an application of Isaiah 53:4. Its language is ambiguous, relating to the sufferings and sorrows of sinful people. While the Servant was 'wounded for our transgressions' (Isaiah 53:5), taking the guilt of the sinful *upon* himself, Matthew sees Jesus *taking away* the sufferings of disease from people. Doubtless he also related this to the gentle ministry of the Servant, over against the clamorous would-be-deliverers of Israel, as he again notes in 12:18–21.

The encounter of the young man with Jesus in 18–20 is well placed after a citation from Isaiah 53; for the Son of man who has nowhere to lay his head is the Servant of the Lord who shares the lot of the suffering poor, and who labours to bring the kingdom of God to the world at the cost of his life (Luke places the episode at the beginning of Jesus's final journey to Jerusalem (Luke 9:57, 58). The one who asked to go and bury his father (21) may have lost his father in death, but that is unlikely, since he would hardly go out prior to the burial; more likely he expressed the desire to care for his father until his death – then he would follow Jesus ('I must bury my father' was said by a Syrian to one who advised him to get a university education). The answer of Jesus is not to release a man from responsibility to parents (contrast Mark 7:9–13), but to emphasise the priority of the kingdom of God over all human ties, including the dearest. What Jesus demanded he did himself – and carried it through to his last breath.

TO THINK ABOUT: God *first* – today, and in all my tomorrows.

8:23–34 The stilling of two tempests

The account of the stilling of the storm by Jesus has instructive over-tones. The Lake of Galilee, surrounded by hills with ravines, is subject to violent storms. This one must have been unusually great for experienced fishermen to be afraid for their lives (Matthew describes it in v. 24 as 'a great earthquake in the sea'). The awe of the disciples at the calm which followed the command of Jesus is the more comprehensible. Jewish Christians reflecting on the narrative would recall that, in the Old Testament, supremacy over the turbulent sea was a mark of the power of the almighty creator (see, for example, Job 38:8–11; Ps. 29:10), thus his victory over hostile forces is depicted in terms of rebuking raging waters (Isa. 17:12–14). That same power of God is active in Jesus who is able to still all our 'storms' in the present, and it will work through him to still the final storms of history (compare Luke 21:25–28).

The storm on the lake is reflected in the storm within the demoniacs of Gadara (or Gergesa, the manuscript tradition in v. 28 is uncertain; if 'Gadara' is correct, it will denote the territory between Gadara and the lake). The cry in v. 29 reflects a recognition that the coming of the Messiah in his kingdom brings to an end the affliction of mankind by evil powers (see Matt. 12:28–29); the protest is that he has come too soon! That Jesus should allow demonic powers to impel a herd of pigs to rush into the lake has caused puzzlement. Adolf Schlatter pointed out that the demonic work of destruction in the herd will have demonstrated to the possessed men that they really had been freed from the presence and power of the demons, and he added: 'If the spirits destroy swine, that does not disturb the heart of Jesus, but if they destroy men, he uses his power and drives them away'.

TO THINK ABOUT: 'The story teaches that evil is self-destructive . . . the power of God is shown even when the evil forces have their own way' (Alan Richardson).

Questions for further study and discussion on Matthew 6:9–8:34

1. How does 6:14–15 relate to the unconditional offer of forgiveness through the gospel?

2. Is there a place for fasting in our church and individual lives today? If so, what occasions call for it, and why?

3. Can the thought of 6:19–34 be squared with insurance policies and savings accounts?

4. To what extent can the pressure of a busy life-style become a 'master' (6:24)? How can increasing alienation from the Lord be avoided?

5. Give some contemporary examples to illustrate the principles of 7:1–5.

6. How can we know when to 'give up' with showing a person the things of God? What factors should we take into account first (7:6)?

7. What parallels are there, if any, between the narrative of 8:5–13, the faith of third-world believers and the attitudes typical of 'old world' believers?

8. What application of 8:18–22 is conceivable for disciples today?

9:1–8 Authority to forgive

Matthew's mode of abbreviating a story is very marked in this account, set in Capernaum (now viewed as Jesus's 'own city', see Mark 2:1). All reference to Jesus teaching in a crowded house, and the desperate action of the four friends in tearing a hole in the roof to let down their friend before Jesus, is omitted. Nevertheless the essential words of Jesus and the dialogue and action to which they led, are plainly recorded.

Why did Jesus tell the man, 'Your sins are forgiven', instead of speaking directly to his physical condition? It could have been due to the sick man's assumption that his illness was a punishment for his sins; or to Jesus's knowledge that the paralysis was, in fact, due to a deep sense of guilt; or to the man's awakened sense of guilt in the presence of Jesus (compare Luke 5:8). At all events, Jesus treated the need for forgiveness as greater than that of physical healing, and so he spoke the word of release. That brought instant reaction from the scribes – a charge of blasphemy, on the conviction that God is the sole judge of men and he alone can pronounce them free from guilt. Jesus's response requires reflection on our part. Which indeed is the easier thing to say to a paralysed man? 'Your sins are forgiven', or 'Rise and walk'? We may well be inclined to view the former as easier, for none could disprove its truth, whereas the latter could easily reveal the speaker's ineffectiveness. To a Jew both statements would have been equally pointless, since only God can forgive sins, and only God can make a paralytic walk in an instant. The language of Jesus in v. 6 implies the priority of forgiveness; the divinely authorised power to heal a paralytic at a word reveals the divinely authorised power of the Son of man to declare forgiveness of sins. It is an anticipation of the pronouncement of the Son of man in the last day (compare Matt. 10:32–33).

That the crowd glorified God for giving such authority to *men* (8) may be a generalised statement relating to Jesus in particular ('Son of man' could have been understood by them as simply denoting a man). Matthew will have recorded it with a recognition that like authority was given by Jesus to his followers to declare the forgiveness of sins to those who accept the gospel of Christ. The same meaning is contained in the statements in 16:19 and 18:18.

TO THINK ABOUT: 'There are no degrees in forgiveness. There are degrees in the holiness that follows forgiveness; but pardon must be perfect at its birth. Forgiveness restores each man to the place he had before he fell' (George Matheson).

9:9–17 The Messiah for sinners

The call of Matthew and its aftermath is a revelation of the nature of our Lord's entire ministry. 'Tax collectors and sinners' is a standing phrase in the Gospels. None so well represented the 'sinners' as the tax collectors who, in everyone's estimate, were far from the law, far from God, and far from their own people. But Jesus calls one of them to be an associate in his ministry! And then he goes to his house and joins *many* tax collectors and sinners for a feast! That he should not only mix with these people but eat with them was a living denial of the religion dominated by observation of the ceremonial law. The Pharisees' indignant question in v. 11 is answered in the classic words of 12–13: Jesus was sent precisely to the 'sick'; God's call for mercy (better 'grace' Hos. 6:6) above all religious duties was the guiding principle of his action; and he came to 'call', i.e. invite to the feast of God's kingdom, those who recognised their need for forgiveness. There is an implied warning here lest the vaunted righteousness of the righteous shut them out of the kingdom for sinners.

The question about fasting in 14–15 arises from the zeal for fasting in the time of Jesus, which has been described as 'very nearly obsessive'. In answer to the question why his disciples do not fast, Jesus points out that wedding guests do not fast while a bridegroom is with them in the marriage festivities; his disciples similarly do not fast, because *the bridegroom is with them.* The underlying assumption is breathtaking: Jesus is the Bridegroom-messiah, whose coming introduces the time of salvation, and his friends are *now* enjoying the messianic feast! True, the time approaches when he will be 'taken away' (an echo of Isa. 53:8), and at his death his friends will fast. But their grief will be speedily turned to joy (John 16:16–22), for they will never lose his presence again. The implication is clear: fasting is not a characteristic expression of the friends of the bridegroom in the kingdom he has brought.

TO THINK ABOUT: Life in the new age calls for new 'clothes' (16), as new wine calls for new wineskins (17). How far does my way of life reflect the revolutionary character of the new creation introduced by the revolutionary redeemer? Consider in this connection 2 Corinthians 5:17.

9:18–26 Two examples of faith

These incidents are better known to us from Mark's account. We learn from him that the ruler was Jairus, and that he was a ruler of the synagogue – a prominent position in a Jewish town where life revolved around the synagogue. Matthew's compression of narrative does not allow him to describe the two stages of Jairus's dealing with Jesus: Jairus went to Jesus to implore his aid for his daughter, who was at the point of death; but while on his way back to his house a message came through that she had died (Mark 5:22,35). Jairus had come to Jesus in faith; now he was called on to maintain it in an apparently impossible situation. By contrast, his relatives had none of his faith, so they sent for flute-players to play for the funeral.

What did Jesus mean when he dismissed the musicians with the words, 'The girl is not dead but sleeping'? Either he knew that the child had not really died but was in a coma, and so the miracle was one of supernatural knowledge on his part and restoring a child at the point of death; or he refused to call that death which he was on his way to overcoming. The latter is the unquestionable understanding of the evangelists. Compare our Lord's words about Lazarus: This illness is not to death; it is for the glory of God (John 11:4); 'Our friend Lazarus has fallen asleep, but I go to awake him out of sleep' (11); and then, 'Lazarus is dead . . . but let us go to him' (14). For the Christian death is not the eternal sleep feared by the pagan, but a temporary closing of eyes from which there is to be a glorious awakening by the Conqueror of death (compare 1 Cor. 15:51).

The woman who suffered from a haemorrhage knew something of the isolation of the leper; her condition cut her off from society as perpetually 'unclean'. She manifested a faith which was both primitive and desperate. The only way she dared to attempt to contact the Lord was by clutching a tassel of his robe (compare Num. 15:37–41). This was, to say the least, faith on its lowest level (as late as the time of James I of England women were known to be crushed in their endeavours to touch the king's clothes). But God was merciful to her. The Lord sent her away with even more than she asked: in good heart, in peace, and with an experience of saving grace (22, compare Mark 5:34).

FOR FAITH TODAY: The healing of his seamless dress
                   Is by our beds of pain;
                   We touch him in life's throng and press
                   And we are whole again.
                                        (J. G. Whittier)

9:27–38 God's harvest fields

Matthew now brings to a close his review of the miraculous deeds of the Christ. He has brought together examples of the varied miracles of Jesus: the healing of a leper, of a soldier's boy at a distance, of the fever of Peter's mother-in-law, of a paralytic, of a haemorrhaging woman, the raising of a child from death, and an example of the Lord's power over nature. In our passage he completes it by adding examples of Jesus healing blindness (27–31) and a demoniac who was dumb (32–33). These last two accounts probably have Isaiah 35:4–7 in view, part of the description of God's miraculous deeds in the last days: 'Then the eyes of the blind shall be opened, and the ears of the deaf unstopped . . . and the tongue of the dumb shall sing for joy'. These signs of the coming of God to bring his kingdom of salvation are fulfilled through the Christ whom he has sent.

The conclusion of the review is itself followed by another summary statement of this stage of the ministry of Jesus (35), reminiscent of 4:23. That in turn leads to an observation of our Lord's compassion towards his people (36) and a statement on the current situation, both of which prepare for the account of the mission of the disciples which follows in chapter 10.

Verses 36 and 37 ring a multitude of bells for Old Testament readers. With v. 36 compare the concern of Moses that the people should not be like a flock without a shepherd (Num. 27:17); the vision of Israel like sheep scattered without a shepherd because its king had been slain (1 Kings 22:17); and Ezekiel's condemnation of Israel's 'shepherds' (their rulers), whose neglect of the flock caused the sheep to be scattered over the mountains, so that God undertakes to be their shepherd and to send his servant David to care for them (Ezek. 34). Here was the impulse for the ministry of Jesus to seek and save the lost (Luke 19:10). Verse 37 recalls the biblical use of the metaphor of harvest as the reaping of the ages and the coming of the kingdom of God (see especially Joel 3:11–14). God's hour has struck. The harvest has been prepared for through the sowing by Israel's prophets, culminating in the work of John the Baptist. Now the King himself has come and is redemptively at work, but there is need for more labourers to join in the reaping. The disciples are told to pray for such workers – and are then sent out to be part of the answer to their prayers!

A PRAYER:
  As labourers in thy vineyard, send us out, Christ, to be
    Content to bear the burden of weary days for thee.
  We ask no other wages, when thou shalt call us home,
    But to have shared the travail that makes thy kingdom come.
                                                    (J. S. B. Monsell)

10:1–15 Disciples on mission

We have noted how frequently Matthew abbreviates Mark's narrative. In his discourses he does the opposite. Whereas Mark gives the barest details of the sending of the twelve to Israel (Mark 6:7–13), Matthew expands Mark's brief account with related sayings, so that the church may have a full account of what Jesus taught about mission and so be able to carry out the continuing mission committed to it (Matt. 28:18–20).

The disciples are invested with authority to engage in the same mission that Jesus has received; they are to do his works and preach the same gospel (compare 9:35 with 10:1,7,9). They must also limit their mission to Israel, as Jesus did (5–6), for Jesus was sent to fulfil the promises given to the chosen people in the Old Testament; the time of the Gentiles comes only when the redemptive action for the whole world has been completed in the cross and resurrection (compare Rom. 15:8–9). The other side of that coin is Israel's slowness in responding to the gospel of Christ. All too many Jews assumed that the kingdom was exclusively for them; Jesus sends the disciples to preach the gospel to his people lest they miss the kingdom and the multitudes they despise inherit it (compare Matt. 8:11–12).

This is emphasised in 11–15. The disciples on mission are to ask a householder whether he will receive them and their message (11). The customary greeting of peace ('Shalom!') is to be given, which becomes a blessed reality when the message is accepted; when it is not, the blessing 'returns', for disciples remain in the peace forfeited by the rejectors (13). Where a town rejects the message the disciples are to do what Jews do when they leave Gentile areas and enter the holy land: shake from their feet the dust of the 'unclean' country; for *Jews who reject the gospel of God become pagans!* Yet worse: in Jewish eyes Sodom and Gomorrah were amongst the most wicked cities of all time and its inhabitants were to have no part in the world to come; Jesus declares that there is more hope for Sodom and Gomorrah than for the people of God who reject the gospel of God (15).

TO THINK ABOUT: It is a grave responsibility both to make known the eternal gospel and to hear it. The former requires *very* responsible proclamation, the latter *very* responsible hearing.

10:16–23 Enduring hardship for the gospel

The substance of 17–22 appears in Mark 13:9–13 and is largely repeated in Matthew 24:9–14. Clearly mission in the period after the death of Jesus is in view. Intense opposition by authorities to the preaching of the gospel (17–20) is matched by opposition within families to members accepting the gospel (21–22). The extraordinary deduction of Albert Schweitzer from v. 23, that Jesus expected his exaltation and appearing in glory before the disciples returned from their mission trip, is plainly irreconcilable with the situation depicted.

The disciples are to go out like sheep among wolves, but not to be senseless; they are to combine the proverbial smartness of snakes with the innocence of doves (16 – disciples who are clever without innocence, or innocent without wisdom, will run into trouble!). Observe the repetition in vs. 17,19,21 of the term 'deliver (up)'; it is used in relation to Jesus being delivered up to death (compare 17:22), whether by the agency of men or by God (Rom. 4:25); the disciples in their mission are called to tread the path of Jesus – by permission of God. The parallel extends to the authorities before whom they are to appear: sanhedrins, including that at Jerusalem, synagogues, governors like Pilate, kings like Herod (17–18). Such occasions are to be used as opportunities for testimony to the gospel. The book of Acts illustrates again and again how the disciples put this principle into action (see especially chapters 4,7,22,26). They will not, however, be left to their own resources, for the Holy Spirit will inspire their testimony (20). This promise is amplified in the sayings about the Spirit in John 14–16, who is Counsellor and Advocate.

Verse 23 sheds a grim light on the difficulties ahead in the task of evangelising Israel. Opposition to the gospel will be persistent but the disciples are not to court martyrdom; when opposed they are to go on to other places. The expression 'you will not have gone through' Israel's towns is paraphrastic; read rather, 'you will not have *completed* . . .'; the term denotes the accomplishment of a task. Jesus declares that the task of evangelising Israel will not be completed till his coming at the end. But then it will be (Matt. 23:39).

TO THINK ABOUT – an illustration: 'In this year the Lord's truth was finely planted over the nation, and many thousands were turned to the Lord; insomuch that there were seldom fewer than one thousand in prison in this nation for truth's testimony' (George Fox).

10:24–42 Mission that divides

Verses 24–25 have instructive repetitions and application in John 13:16 and 15:20. Beelzebul (not Beelzebub, 2 Kings 1:2) is a variant for Baal-zeboul, 'Lord of the (lofty) dwelling', a title more fit for God than the devil but probably reflecting the concept of 'prince of the power of the air' of Ephesians 2:2. Verse 26 provides an example of the different ways in which the same saying can be used (compare Mark 4:22, Luke 12:2); its primary application is to the revelation of right and wrong at the judgement. The exhortation of v. 28 is to fear man less and fear *God* more, for God alone has power to exercise the supreme judgement on man (Jas. 4:12); the devil is to be fought, not feared (Jas. 4:7; 1 Pet. 5:8–9). The confession or denial of Jesus before men and corresponding confession or denial of men before God in 32–33 probably has courts of judgement in view – on earth and in heaven; but the principle would apply to confession or denial of Christ anywhere.

'I have not come to bring peace, but a sword' (34) should be compared with John 12:47 and John 9:39 ('I did not come to judge the world . . .'; 'For judgement I came into this world . . .'). The word of the kingdom has an inevitable corollary of judgement, as the hearers of the word divide into believers and rejectors. Nowhere is that division more keenly felt than in families (especially among Jews); the gospel brings about the division declared in Micah 7:6, but faithfulness demands endurance of this as if it were a cross to be carried after Jesus (38).

Verse 40 applies the Jewish principle of apostleship to disciples on mission: 'One who is sent is as he who sent him'. Conjoined with Luke 10:16 the parallelism is positive and negative:

'He who receives you receives me, and he who receives me receives him who sent me.

He who rejects you rejects me, and he who rejects me rejects him who sent me.'

The authorisation is complete, and calls for authoritative witness. The discourse ends with assurance of reward for all who assist in the work of the mission (41,42).

TO THINK ABOUT: 'Reward is always based only on the kindness of God, who takes our actions so seriously that he does not forget the slightest deed which has been done for him' (Eduard Schweizer).

Questions for further study and discussion on Matthew 9,10

1. What lessons for today's church can be drawn from our Lord's concern for 'outsiders', and the Pharisees' resistance to it?

2. How would you describe faith, in the light of 9:18–26?

3. Has Matthew 9–10 any significance for the church's ministry to those who are suffering today?

4. What conceivable relevance has 10:5–15 for the modern Gentile church?

5. Does 10:40 apply to apostles, or ordained clergy, or all believers?

6. How was the disciples' prayer of 9:38 answered? In what ways have you found prayer to be just the beginning of action on your part? Give specific examples.

7. What should our attitude to our family be if we find that we are the only Christian and that the others resent our faith (see 10:34–38 and compare with Romans 12:14–18)?

11:1–15 Jesus, John and the kingdom of God

John the Baptist, languishing in prison, sends a message to Jesus, asking whether he were 'the Coming One', or whether they had to look for another. The reason for the message is clear: John had proclaimed the coming of the mighty Messiah who should bring God's judgement and reveal the kingdom in power. This he looked for Jesus to do, but instead of executing judgement on the wicked Jesus was spending his time preaching and mixing with people of doubtful morals: when was the real action going to begin? Or was that beyond the power of Jesus? The Lord kept the messengers beside him for the day, and then sent them back with a message (5) which embodied the central part of Isaiah 35: what God had promised to do in the day of his coming for the kingdom was now taking place through Jesus. *That* gave the answer to John's question!

Jesus's tribute to John follows. John is 'more than a prophet'; he is the 'messenger' who prepares the Lord's way (Mal. 3:1); he has fulfilled the role of the returning Elijah (Mal. 4:5); he is the greatest of those born of women. But, adds Jesus astonishingly, 'he who is least in the kingdom of heaven is greater than he'. For John prepared the way for others to enter the kingdom, but is not one of those standing with Jesus in it. Light is thrown on this in the enigmatic v. 12. The rendering in the RSV margin has been adopted in the text of the NIV: 'the kingdom of heaven has been *forcefully advancing*' (rather than 'suffering violence'). The underlying Aramaic (and Hebrew) term used by Jesus (*parash*) is used of an army making a breach through a city wall under attack, and it enables a word play thus:

From the days of John the Baptist until now
the kingdom of heaven *has made a powerful breach* into the world,
and violent men are *making a powerful assault* upon it.

John's ministry served to introduce the period of God's kingly work of salvation; through Jesus it is pressing forward in great power; the opposition has silenced John in prison, and is turning against Jesus. But the opposition is overplaying its hand for, through the suffering Christ, the kingdom will come in yet greater power and will be opened for the whole world.

TO THINK ABOUT: For subsequent followers of the Lamb, 'The outcome of the battle may be sure, but the casualties are going to be real, not sham' (N. Perrin).

11:16–24 A truculent generation

By parable and by prophetic warning Jesus condemns the unresponsiveness of his generation to the word of God. First, his contemporaries are compared to quarrelsome children who blame their playmates for not playing the games that they wanted. The key to the interpretation appears to be that the complaining children are *sitting*. They are literally 'calling the tune'. The boys want to play the pipe for weddings (it is men who participate in the round dance at a wedding), whereas the girls want to sing the mourners' dirges, and the *other* children are called on to do the dancing and to act out the funeral. The people of 'this generation' are the children who reproach the others for not doing as they want them to do. Jesus implies: 'God sends you his messengers, but all you do is to give orders and criticise. You hate the preaching of repentance, and you hate the proclamation of the gospel' (so J. Jeremias).

The use of the expression 'Son of man' in v. 19 is an example where it is ambiguous; it can mean simply '(a) man', or even 'I', or it can denote the representative of God's kingdom, as in Dan. 7:13; those with seeing eyes and hearing ears can perceive the meaning in view. Here the comparison between Jesus and John is not simply between an ascetic prophet and one who shares fellowship with others, but between two complementary missions in relation to the kingdom of God. Different as they were, John and Jesus were both God's emissaries with crucial roles in the bringing of God's kingdom of salvation to men, but their contemporaries were too blind to perceive it in either.

Although this rejection of Jesus and John is illuminated by a parable of quarrelsome children, the issues were infinitely more serious than childish folly. The men of this generation had refused God's ultimate message for mankind; accordingly the judgement of God was inescapable. For the comparison with Tyre and Sidon in 21–24, see the prophecies against these nations in Ezekiel 26:1–28:23. The judgement pronounced on Capernaum in v. 23 echoes that declared against the prince of Tyre in Ezekiel 28:8.

TO THINK ABOUT: 'There are only two kinds of people in the end: those who say to God, "Thy will be done", and those to whom God says, in the end, "*Thy* will be done" ' (C. S. Lewis).

11:25–30 The great thanksgiving

This passage is one of the great declarations of the New Testament concerning the identity and the task of our Lord. Luke has 25–26 in a different context (Luke 10:21–22), but sufficiently related to enable us to understand what 'these things' are that are hidden from the wise and intelligent and revealed to 'babes': they are the realities of the kingdom of God that show its presence in Jesus (compare Matt. 11:2–5, 10–15). Jesus thanks his Father for revealing them to people who, though infants in understanding, open their heart to his word; and equally for *hiding* them from those whose hardness of heart leads them to resist the truth. Paul reflects the same thought in 1 Corinthians 1:18–31 where Jesus is spoken of as God's wisdom for man, a concept which lies at the basis of the following verses.

To a remarkable extent v. 27 reflects the central teaching of the Gospel of John concerning the relation of Jesus to God. While Jesus often speaks of God as Father, there is only one other passage in the first three Gospels in which the absolute terms 'the Son', 'the Father', occur, namely Matthew 24:36 paralleled in Mark 13:32, where again the Son is set over against all mankind in relation to God. In this context it is evident that the deliverance of 'all things' to the Son denotes *all things revealed* to him for man (contrast the 'all things' of 28:18). This is based on a unique mutual knowledge of the Father and the Son; in the Bible 'knowledge' has to do with relationship (John 17:3; in Amos 3:2 it denotes covenant relationship). Out of this unique relationship Jesus invites people to come under the saving rule of God, and so participate in the fellowship with the Father which he enjoys.

There is an instructive parallel to 28–30 in Ecclesiasticus 51:23–30, where the writer invites all to benefit from his acquirement of wisdom: 'Come to me, you who need instruction, and lodge in my house of learning . . . Put your neck under the yoke, be ready to accept discipline . . . Do your duty in good time, and in his own time he (God) will reward you'. There speaks a Sadducee. Jesus, from the Father's heart, invites people burdened with the heavy joke of the law (compare Matt. 23:4; Acts 15:10) to accept his yoke, which is the yoke of the kingdom of God. It is 'easy', for it fits man just as he is, and it brings him who wears it redemption from the powers of sin; rest of soul; and the life of God's new world.

FOR MEDITATION: I love thy yoke to wear,
                  To feel thy gracious bands –
                  Sweetly restrained by thy care,
                  And happy in thy hands.
                                          (T. H. Gill)

12:1–8 The Lord of the sabbath

Chapter 12 recounts a series of confrontations between Jesus and the Jewish teachers, whereby we see how the division between them became a gulf as the Pharisees increased their attacks on him.

Plucking corn in someone else's field was allowed by the law (Deut. 23:25) – but not on the sabbath. In the eyes of the Jews plucking ears of corn amounted to reaping, and rubbing them in the hands was threshing. Whereas we are inclined to say, 'Rubbish!' Jesus did not dispute their interpretation. Instead he cited an occasion from the Old Testament when human need took precedence over legal requirements (1 Sam. 21:1–6) and pointed out that priestly service in the temple continually demanded sabbath work. This he followed by three comments: (1) 'Something greater than the temple is here', i.e. the kingdom of God operative in Jesus (remember that 'kingdom of God' for a Jew meant 'God sovereignly *active*'!); (2) the word of God shows that mercy has priority over legal enactments (Hos. 6:6); (3) 'The Son of man is lord of the sabbath'. In this last statement Matthew has compressed Mark, who places before the dictum the famous saying, 'The sabbath was made for man, not man for the sabbath', and he continues, '*so* the Son of man is lord even of the sabbath'. In this last sentence '*even* of' should probably be rendered '*also* of the sabbath' (it is the ordinary word 'and'). We then ask, '*In addition to what* is the Son of man lord of the sabbath?' The answer is found in Genesis 1:28, 'Have dominion over the fish of the sea . . . the birds of the air . . . every living thing that moves . . .' As man was set over the creatures which God made in the six days of creation, so he was intended to exercise sovereignty over the sabbath also, i.e. through his sovereign use of the sabbath for God's glory. But man is fallen! His sovereignty over creation is incomplete, for he cannot even rule over himself. But Jesus, the Son of man, has come, the representative of man and mediator of the saving sovereignty of God, in order to redeem man from the powers that enslave him and so restore him to the destiny for which he was created. The argument is precisely paralleled by the use of Psalm 8 in Hebrews 2:5–9. The transition from man in relation to creation to the Son of man in relation to the saving rule of God is natural in view of the fact that, among the Jews, the sabbath was seen as a type and anticipation of the kingdom of God (compare Heb. 4).

TO THINK ABOUT: 'If the Son makes you free, you will be free indeed' (John 8:36). 'For freedom Christ has set us free; stand fast therefore, and do not submit again to a yoke of slavery' (Gal. 5:1).

12:9–21 A crucial sabbath healing

The presence of a disabled man in a synagogue on the sabbath day gave an opportunity for opponents of Jesus to raise the question of v. 10. It was a serious issue for, according to Exodus 31:14, sabbath breaking was a capital offence. Everyone knew the attitude of Jesus to sick people. They also knew the Jewish rule that help was allowable to one in danger of death on the sabbath, but the crippled man did not fall into that category. How should Jesus answer the question? He responds by a counter question: Which man in the congregation will not lift out a sheep of his that has fallen into a pit on the sabbath? In reality Jews differed on that one. Some said that if the animal would survive if given food, it could have it and be pulled out after the Sabbath. Others said that a mattress could be put under the animal so that it could get out by its own exertions. Others (like the Qumran sectaries) maintained that to take *any* action was contrary to the law. Jesus assumes that the majority would do something for the animal (who wants to lose a sheep, anyway?) and, in the typical Jewish manner of arguing from the lesser to the greater, he comments, 'How much more valuable is a man than a sheep!' From this he deduced a principle that went beyond anything his hearers were willing to admit: 'So then *it is lawful to do good on the sabbath*'. Jesus then healed the man, illustrating again the maxim earlier cited from Hosea 6:6: God wills that man should at all times act in the spirit of divine mercy and not make the law a hindrance to such action.

The response of the Pharisees was to go out and plan the death of Jesus (14). A shocking reaction to a miracle of divine mercy! Jesus therefore 'withdrew from there' – and from ministry in the synagogue. In this Matthew sees a fulfilment of the first song of the Servant of God (Isa. 42:1–4). The act of withdrawal and the repressing of excitement over his cures (16) relates to Isaiah 42:3–4a. Matthew was also conscious that, through his witnesses, the crucified and risen Lord was proclaiming justice to the Gentiles (18). He was in the process of bringing justice to victory (20), and the Gentiles were putting their hope in his name (21) in anticipation of the time when God's kingdom will be victorious over all.

A PRAYER: O Jesus Christ, you were willing to bear scorn that the despised might have your friendship, and a cross that the guilty might have love: Let your Spirit live in me, for I depend on your strength and love; some may depend today on mine.

12:22–37 Jesus – from heaven or hell?

The charge that Jesus was in league with the devil – 'the prince of the demons' (24) – is important as evidence that even the enemies of Jesus could not deny his mighty works. The man in the street was beginning to think that he must be the Messiah, the 'Son of David' (23). In seeking to dissuade people from that conclusion the Pharisees could not deny that Jesus was doing works beyond the power of man, so they asserted that he must be inspired by the devil.

Jesus in reply adduces a variety of issues:

1. A kingdom torn by civil war, or a clan rent by internal strife, is heading for destruction; if Satan is inspiring a force against himself he is destroying his own kingdom (25–26). Not even the devil is as stupid as that!

2. The Pharisees themselves at times exorcised the possessed, admittedly not on the scale of the works of Jesus, so were they also in league with the devil? The question was the more important since it was not the young but the *leaders* of the Pharisees who attempted these works (27).

3. If it was by God's Spirit, not Satan, that Jesus overcame the demonic powers, then the kingdom of God that conquers Satan's kingdom had come among them – and they were thrusting that salvation from themselves (28).

4. These actions demonstrated that Satan was a defeated power, admittedly powerful, but overcome by someone stronger (29; compare Isa.49:24–25) indicating that God was fulfilling his promise of victory through Jesus.

5. A grave consequence followed from these considerations: in their allegations the Pharisees were guilty of blasphemy against the Holy Spirit, for they were identifying God's work in the world with the devil's (31–32). They were manifesting an antipathy towards God and so were placing themselves beyond forgiveness, resisting the only one who could give them forgiveness and life; their unholy words proceeded from an inward corruption for which they must answer on the last day (33–37). It goes without saying that such a condemnation does not relate to sensitive souls who fear that they may have sinned in this way, but to the hardened who recognise and resist the Christ, the Spirit, and the Father who sends them.

A PRAYER: Give me, O Lord, a steadfast heart, which no unworthy affection may drag downwards; an unconquered heart, which no tribulation can wear out; an upright heart, which no unworthy purpose may tempt aside. (Thomas Aquinas)

12:38–50 The sign of Jonah

The request for a sign from Jesus, reported in v. 38, was presumably not coincident in time with the controversy of 22–37 (Mark, 8:11, and Luke, 11:29, place it later). Such a demand would not have appeared unreasonable to Jews, in the light of Deuteronomy 13:1–5. But in view of the ability of false prophets to deceive, the rabbis stated that the sign required by this passage had to be 'in heaven'. That is what these Jews were seeking: an apocalyptic wonder in heaven, for miracles on earth can be produced by demonic powers (see Luke 11:15–16). The response of Jesus in v. 39 is uncompromising: this generation is 'evil and adulterous' since it rejects both the message he brings from God concerning his kingdom, and the deeds in which it was being manifested, seeking instead yet other signs. No such sign, he said, would be given; only 'the sign of Jonah' (39). In Luke 11:30 this is expounded, 'For as Jonah became a sign to the men of Nineveh, so will the Son of man be to this generation'. The explanation in Matthew 12:40 is entirely in harmony with the contemporary understanding of Jonah and with the statements of the book itself: the sign of Jonah is the miracle of his deliverance from death, which was comparable to a resurrection (observe the prayer in Jonah 2: the belly of the whale is paralleled with the belly of Sheol, v. 2; with the heart of the seas, v. 3; and with the pit where the bars of the underworld closed over Jonah 'for ever', v. 6. Note, too, Jonah's thanksgiving, 'Thou didst bring up my life from the pit, O Lord my God', v. 6).

When Matthew recorded vs. 40–42 he doubtless would have recognised that the successors of Jesus's generation continued the sin of their predecessors, in that they rejected even *this* sign (compare Luke 16:31); the words of Jesus were doubly confirmed.

The meaning of the parable of the cleansed 'house' (43–45) was that superficial repentance is not enough; if it is not followed by opening to the *Holy* Spirit a worse relapse takes place. The saying in 49–50 defines the true family of Jesus; in a secondary manner it reflects the kind of renunciation which he had already urged on his disciples (10:37), but one still wholly compatible with love (compare John 19:26,27).

TWO COMPLEMENTARY COMMENTS:
'He does not scorn his mother, but he places his Father before her' (J. A. Bengel).
'Christian faith soon proves that it is not the breach but the safeguard of human love' (G. Buttrick).

Questions for further study and discussion on Matthew 11–12

1. What signs of the kingdom of God are observable in our time?

2. Consider objections to the Christian faith in the light of 11:16–18.

3. Compare the sabbath with the Lord's Day, and compare the principles that govern the observance of each.

4. What place should miracles have in gospel proclamation to a secular society?

5. How can one help a person convinced that he or she has committed the 'unforgivable' sin?

6. How would you reply to someone who asked you how they could be sure (like John in 11:2–3) that Jesus really was the son of God?

7. The people of John the Baptist's time had a variety of opinions and examples of what a 'man of God' should be. What do you expect of a 'full-time Christian worker' in terms of character and lifestyle – and how do *you* match up to these expectancies?

8. God was evidently 'excited' about the life of his son, Jesus. What do you suppose it was that God 'delighted in' with regard to Jesus's life (12:18–21)? What of Jesus's life can be reflected in ours?

13:1–9, 18–23 The parable of the sower

Chapter 13 is the third great discourse of Matthew, consisting of seven parables of Jesus concerning the kingdom of God. The first is the best known and most disputed of the seven. No less than four different features of the parable have been claimed to provide its chief point of emphasis: the sower, the soils, the seed, the harvest. It is difficult to deny the importance of any of these – and there is no need to. While it is true that a parable commonly has a single point of emphasis, here is one in which there is at least one main point, and several subsidiary points along with it.

The picture is clear. A Palestinian farmer sows his field, but unlike his western counterparts he does not first plough and then sow; he sows the entire field, paths as well, and then ploughs it all in. What has Jesus in view in the comparison of sowing and reaping? As a parable of the kingdom it appears to be a depiction of *the mission of the kingdom of God*: its operation in the world, proclaimed in word and enacted, opposed in a variety of ways but, in spite of all setbacks, coming with fullness of blessing (note that the three situations of waste and failure: through birds, shallow soil and thorns, are balanced by three situations of success: thirty-, sixty- and a hundred-fold). The parable portrays the inevitability of obstacles to the work of the kingdom, for it is a fallen world to which the kingdom comes. Resistance, disappointments and hardships belong to the context of the Lord's work, as truly as devouring birds, weeds, scorching heat and downtrodden paths are part and parcel of a farmer's toil. But one must never deduce, as some have from this parable, that 'the normal result of God's word is *failure!*' (J. Schniewind), or that it teaches 'the unspeakable tragedy of almightly truth and love, *doomed for the most part to sterility*' (R. Guardini). The harvest which will be gathered will make up God's glorious kingdom, to the coming of which he guides all history. The challenge of the parable is whether we shall be among those who will be part of that harvest (so in the application of the parable, 18–23). Meanwhile, let none be dismayed by the difficulties of kingdom work; be realistic, yes, but recognise that God is working his purpose out to its appointed end. So this parable may be read as encouragement for the discouraged evangelist, as a call to the uncommitted for faith, and as a spur to the half-hearted for genuine dedication.

A PRAYER: O faithful Lord, teach us to trust thee for life and death, and to take thee for our All in All. (Tersteegen)

13:10–17 The reason for parables

Parables are as characteristic to the teaching of Jesus as his deeds of power to his action. In v. 34 Matthew writes, 'Jesus . . . said nothing to them without a parable'. In answer to the question why he does this (10) several points are made:

1. 'To you it has been given to know the secrets of the kingdom of heaven' (11). Mark has the singular term, 'secret' (Mark 4:11), but the difference is not great. Matthew speaks of the meaning of the varied parables of Jesus about the kingdom, Mark the fact that they all amount to one: the presence of the kingdom of God in the person and work of Jesus. To grasp that in and through Jesus God is establishing his saving rule is to have the key to his parables.

2. But here is the rub: most in Israel have neither grasped the secret (13) nor responded to its challenge. The parables ought to enable them to perceive the truth, but in Jesus the experience of Isaiah is repeated: 'This people's heart has grown dull . . . lest they turn for me to heal them' (14–15, citing Isa. 6:9–10). The passage in Isaiah has often been viewed as bitter irony, the language of purpose signifying result, but it is more likely that it expresses the judgement of God on the nation which perpetually rejects his call. Predestination and responsibility always go together. So in the time of Jesus the rejection of his message entailed the divine rejection of the nation as nation. But, as in Isaiah's day the hardening of the nation was qualified by the calling of a remnant, so, in that of Jesus, disciples were called as the first fruits of God's universal rule (compare 31–33).

3. In contrast to this unhappy situation, the blessedness of the disciples is affirmed in 16–17, the message of which is clearly stated by T. W. Manson: 'What for all former generations lay still in the future is now a present reality. What was for the best men of the past only an object of faith is now a matter of experience'. The disciples have witnessed the fulfilment of the visions of the prophets in the salvation of the kingdom of God. In the beautiful words of E. Lohmeyer: 'To the question, "How long is the night?" the answer is now given, "The night is past, the day has broken. *It is wedding day!*" ' (Mark 2: 18–19).

A PRAYER: I ask no dream, no prophet-ecstasy,
      No sudden rending of the veil of clay,
    No angel visitant, no opening skies,
      But *take the dimness of my soul away*.
                    (G. Croly)

13:24–30, 36–43 The wheat and the weeds

It is doubtful that any parable of Jesus has been more widely misunderstood than the one before us. The situation depicted is clear enough. A farmer sows his field with grain, and an enemy oversows it with spurious seed. The term 'weeds' in v. 25 is not precise enough; 'darnel' is better, yet more accurately 'bearded wheat'. It was sometimes grown for chicken feed but it creates nausea in humans. Its likeness to ordinary wheat makes it possible for mistakes to be made in sowing, but this instance was no mistake; it was intended to ruin a harvest. The key feature of the parable is the command to the labourers who wished to root out the poisonous growth: 'Let both grow together until the harvest' (30), then the separation will take place.

What is the lesson of the parable? Commonly it has been assumed that 'the kingdom of heaven' in v. 24 is the church, begun by the work of Jesus but from earliest times infiltrated by spurious members (37–38). Whereas enthusiasts are always wanting to eliminate from its midst members suspected of not being true Christians, the Lord forbids premature judgement: 'Let both grow together until the harvest', then he, and he alone, will judge his people (40–43). This interpretation conflicts with v. 38 and with the intention of the parables of growth generally. 'The field is the world', it is said in v. 38, where the kingdom of God has been initiated through Jesus with a view to the harvest of the final kingdom. But a contrary force has been set in motion: an 'enemy' through his agents is endeavouring to ruin the work of God in Christ and to destroy the harvest in advance; one thinks of the attacks of the Pharisees on Jesus, Herod's silencing of John the Baptist in prison, and the whole endeavour gathering momentum to silence Jesus too. What should be done in face of this movement? Call for open resistance to these enemies? All the men of Israel would have rallied to Jesus instantly if he had done that! But the task of Jesus is to bring to the world the saving powers of God's kingdom, not its judgement (John 3:17). God who has sent him has the situation in his hands and he will lead it to its victorious future; not till then will the Son of man be mediator for judgement. 'Let both grow together', then, is a rejection of the impatience of the righteous and a call for the patience of God in the light of his sure victory.

A PRAYER: Lord, thy kingdom bring triumphant,
    Visit us this living hour,
   Let thy toiling, sinning children
    See thy kingdom come in power.
        (A. F. Bayly)

13:31–35,44–46   Mustard seed, leaven, treasure, a pearl

Matthew here relates two pairs of parables, virtually twins, each of the twins conveying an instruction fundamentally similar to the other.

The parables of the mustard seed and the leaven provide two different pictures which emphasise the contrast between the beginning and the end of God's saving sovereignty, mediated through the work of Jesus the Messiah. The mustard seed is very small among household seeds, but it becomes (in Palestine) a very tall plant – 'a midget of a seed among seeds, but a veritable tree among herbs', as C. W. F. Smith put it. Similarly a small amount of leaven mixed with dough makes the whole lump a bubbling mass. The images used emphasise the greatness of the conclusion. The birds nesting in the branches of the tree call to mind this use of the figure in the Old Testament, notably in Daniel 4:10–12, relating to the nations being under the authority of Nebuchadnezzar, and Ezekiel 17:22–24, where the nations of the world come under the rule of God in his kingdom. So also the amount of flour in which the woman puts the leaven is enormous (NIV gives approximate equivalents: half a bushel or twenty-two litres) – enough for a great feast! So we are presented here with an encouraging picture of the ministry of Jesus: though quiet in its beginnings, according to God's will (compare 12:18–21), the almighty power of God is behind it working through it with a view to the glorious end: the completed kingdom. (NB: the frequent use of leaven to depict evil influences must not deflect us from the above interpretation, as though the parables depict an end in corruption. It is the kingdom of *God* in mind, not of the *devil*! For a Jewish example in the spirit of the parable, compare this statement of Rabbi Joshua ben Levi: 'Great is peace, in that peace is to the earth as leaven to the dough'.)

The basic thought of the second pair of parables, the parables of the treasure and the pearl, is 'the incomparable worth of the kingdom of God, which surpasses all earthly things, for which everything must be offered up' (H. D. Wendland). This 'offering', however, is not to be emphasised, for the worth of what is found is such that there's no question of talk about 'sacrifice' to get it, only sheer, unbounded joy. Nevertheless this element in the pictures is a reminder that the two parables do more than supply instruction; they include a call: Let everyone who hears be sure to get the treasure or secure the pearl!

TO THINK ABOUT: 'As soon as your foot is turned to the fields of gold, all heaven is astir to help you. Strange helps will come to you – hints, intuitions, breathings, curious allurements' (Smetham).

13:47–58 The drag-net: Jesus at Nazareth

The likeness of the parable of the drag-net to that of the wheat and the darnel is evident, but there are differences. In the former the idea of separation is stressed. Whereas in the wheat and darnel the alien elements are introduced after the sowing, in the net the different kinds are gathered at the same time, and the sorting is carried out at once. This, however, belongs to the nature of the picture. In a Jewish setting it is unthinkable for fishing with a large net to take place without separating the clean fish from the unclean and inedible; a catch of fish has to be followed by a sorting of fish. We must therefore see *the entire action* of throwing out a net, gathering fish of every kind, drawing in the net and sorting the fish on the shore, as the comparison with the kingdom of heaven. If there is a point of emphasis it is *the gathering of men and women of every kind* through the work of the kingdom. This is what Jesus did in his ministry and what the Jewish leaders thought he had no business to do. But people who object to finding fish of every kind in their net have to stay at home and leave fishing to others! That is exactly what the Jewish leaders did. Jesus, on the contrary, was concerned with fishing on a broad scale and he called his disciples to join him in it. A modern counterpart to this may well be the distaste of Christians generally to taking the gospel to men on 'Skid Row', to disreputable places where Christians would not wish to be seen dead, let alone alive, but where people live and die in their sin. Here is one context where the idea of the church as an *ark* is unsuitable to kingdom work; the Lord wants *fishing boats!*

Was the 'scribe trained for the kingdom of heaven' (52) the author of our Gospel, 'bringing out of his treasure what is new and what is old'? He is apparently a real scribe. As one trained in the law and its exposition he is now able to follow in the footsteps of Jesus and show how the Lord fulfils the law and prophets (5:17).

Nazareth gave no welcome to Jesus (54–57). Had its inhabitants listened to the Pharisees? The question of where Jesus got his wisdom and mighty works from (54) sounds suspiciously as though their answer was *not*, 'from God'. They therefore 'took offence at him', and rejected his message. Nazareth denied its sufferers the opportunity of knowing the power of the kingdom in Jesus (58) and they missed the kingdom themselves.

FOR PRAYER: Pray that your life, your home, your church, and your town may be spared the blighting effect of blindness like Nazareth's.

14:1–12 The death of the forerunner

The account of John's death in 3–12 is inserted at this point in the Gospel to explain the reference to Herod's perplexity about Jesus (1–2); the event had happened earlier (3). Herod will have learned about Jesus in the first instance through his supporters among the Jews (see Mark 3:6). The mission tour of the disciples in his territory will have compelled him to take more notice of the new 'prophet'. The notion that Jesus was John the Baptist risen from the dead (2) was initially a popular rumour among the people, taken up by Herod and repeated by him in his bewilderment (see Mark 6:14–16).

Herod had been rebuked by John for his incestuous marriage to Herodias, the wife of his half-brother Philip (not the tetrarch of that name, Luke 3:1). The rebuke was entirely in line with the role of the Old Testament prophets among their people, but it infuriated Herodias, who sought his death (Mark 6:19). The evangelists will doubtless have perceived the similarity with the situation of the prophet whose anticipated future role John fulfilled, namely Elijah. A weak king, Ahab, was patently afraid of Elijah and helpless to resist him, but his wife, Jezebel, endeavoured to take his life (1 Kings 19:1–3). Where she failed, Herod's 'Jezebel' succeeded. Herod should have refused the spiteful request of Herodias through her daughter, for he had not thought of murder in the promise he made to the girl; in the event the 'greatest among those born of women' was executed to prevent a king losing face. John's death is also paralleled, in two ways, with that of the Lord whose way he prepared: on the one hand in the cruel spite of the persecutors of Jesus, and on the other in the weakness of a ruler who had the power to restrain jealous vindictiveness but failed to do so. The evangelists may have perceived more: they record that as disciples of John took his body and buried it, so a disciple of Jesus, Joseph of Arimathea, requested the body of Jesus and buried it in his own grave (Mark underlines the parallel by using in both cases, for the only time in his Gospel, the unusual term *ptoma*, corpse). It has accordingly been affirmed: 'The Gospel consists of two passion stories – the one ending in death, the other ending in resurrection' (W. Lock). But the second accomplished, with its resurrection, what the first could not: the climax of redemption in the kingdom of God!

A PRAYER: Lord, help me to grow into your likeness, to stand fearlessly for your truth, to love the unlovely, and to forgive those who treat me despitefully.

14:13–21 The Galilean Lord's Supper

The withdrawal by Jesus to a lonely place, mentioned in v. 13, is linked by Mark to the return of the twelve from their mission tour (Mark 6:30–31); Matthew gives the impression that Jesus wished to withdraw from undesirable publicity in view of Herod's actions and interest in him. The two motives are not incompatible. But quietness was not to be gained; the crowds heard of his movements and they thronged to meet him. His compassion met their need, not only for the word and for healing, but also their hunger. What actually happened in that lonely place? Assuredly more than that Jesus persuaded those who had bread to share it with those who had none, as some have suggested. The re-creative power of God present in and with Jesus acted in such fashion as to make available to men and women that which was needed for life, and thereby provided a parable in action of the saving sovereignty which gives life in the kingdom that knows no end. Of the motifs present in the account of the event we mention the following:

1. As Israel was fed with manna in the wilderness under the leadership of Moses, the first Redeemer (so called by the Jews), so Jesus realised the expectation that manna would be given through the second Redeemer, the Messiah, when he came with the kingdom (compare John 6:31–32).

2. The terms he 'took', 'blessed', 'broke', 'gave', are reminiscent of the words and actions of Jesus in the Last Supper; the discourse of John 6 shows how the event may be linked with the continuing celebrations of the Lord's Supper.

3. The compassion of the Lord in the feeding of the crowd made the event an anticipation of the feast of the kingdom of God, of which the Last Supper was promise and pledge (compare Luke 22:29–30); every celebration of the Lord's Supper should be viewed as a foretaste of this.

FOR PRAYER: **Break thou the bread of life, dear Lord, to *me*,**
As thou didst break the bread beside the sea.

Questions for further study and discussion on Matthew 13:1–14:21

1. Consider an appropriate contemporary application of the parable of the sower.

2. What may we learn from the difference in the ways Jesus addressed his disciples and those outside the believing group (13:11,34)?

3. What encouragement can be gained from the parable of wheat and darnel for today's world?

4. A question prompted by 13:44,45, which we need to ask ourselves from time to time is, 'How much does knowledge of Christ and life in the kingdom of heaven really mean to me?' Answer this now for yourself.

5. What does 13:52 indicate about the nature and role of the Old Testament?

6. What does 13:52 indicate about the task of teachers of the Christian faith and of our own study of the Bible?

7. How would you present and explain the feeding miracle to an unbeliever?

14:22–36 The Lord on the waters

That Jesus *made* his disciples get into the boat (22) after the feeding miracle is explained in John 6:15: the crowd was so affected by the event that they tried to force Jesus to become their king. (Some early authorities read there that when Jesus saw what they were doing he *fled* to the hills.) It was a most dangerous moment which threatened to jeopardise his whole ministry, so he removed his disciples from the scene (how they must have revelled in it! How disappointed to have to go!) and he sought communion with his Father for guidance (23).

From his vantage point on the hills Jesus sees the twelve, only half-way across the lake, toiling against the storm. He therefore goes to their aid 'in the fourth watch', i.e. about 3.00 a.m., walking on the waters. The terror of the disciples (26) is comprehensible; in the mountainous seas they would catch only glimpses of him, and thought they were seeing a ghost. Jesus called out words of assurance, which later Christians viewed as significant: 'Take heart, *I am* have no fear!' They remembered the lordship of God over the turbulent waters, as recorded, for example, in Psalm 77:16–19, concluding with the words, 'Thy way was through the sea, thy path through the great waters; yet thy footprints were unseen', and Job's assertion that God 'trampled the waves of the sea' (Job 9:8). The power of God's saving sovereignty was manifest in enabling his Son to go to his people in their distress. The church through the ages has seen in this an anticipation of the way the Lord will come to the aid of his people in the last times; as the church struggles in the mounting waves and contrary winds of opposition, the Lord will come, bringing peace to winds and waves – and to them.

Peter's endeavour to join Jesus on the stormy waters is commonly seen as an acted parable of the apostle's impulsiveness, his daring to launch out in faith, but failure as he looks at the sea instead of to the Lord (compare his later denials), and his rescue by the Lord, as he was later restored after the resurrection.

The whole narrative is for faith. It was no natural event; but neither was Jesus, though real man, an ordinary man, nor was God with him in an ordinary way.

FOR WORSHIP: O where is he that trod the sea?
My soul, the Lord is here!
Let all thy fears be hushed in thee,
Be thine to look and hear.
(C. Wordsworth)

15:1–20 The tradition of the elders

The Pharisees and scribes who came down from Jerusalem (1) were probably a deputation from the religious headquarters to find out just what Jesus was doing. Their fears were confirmed: Jesus did not keep the law! At least, that is how they viewed the position, since for them 'the law' meant the written law as interpreted by the authentic explanations handed down from the dim past. The traditional commentary on the law, described in v. 2 as 'the tradition of the elders', was taught by the scribes, who traced their succession back to Moses and claimed that the teaching was of equal authority to the written law. It was subsequently written down, and formed the Mishnah.

The visitors attacked Jesus via his disciples: Why do they transgress the tradition of the elders by not washing their hands free from ritual defilement before they eat? Jesus countered by another question: Why do you transgress *God's word* by your tradition? He cites an example of this in relation to the command to honour parents. Honour is not a matter of words only, but of actions. A man should support his parents, but the tradition enables a man to escape such obligation. Verse 5 cites a vow formula which may be rendered, 'A gift to God be that which you could receive from me'; but these Jews were using vows merely as forms of words with limited application and so not necessarily binding the speaker to the action declared. In this case the son is not handing over money to the temple authorities, but by his vow is releasing himself from financial obligation to his parents. That is using religious language to evade the command of God and making tradition into a *sinful* tradition. (NB: later Jews prohibited this misuse of vows.) Jesus then presses his attack further: 'Not what goes into the mouth defiles a man, but what comes out of the mouth, this defiles a man' (11). The Pharisees were outraged! For the 'parable' (*mashal*, which means parable, proverb, or riddle) cut at the root of their most characteristic expression of religion – the maintenance of ritual purity. As explained in 17–20, *foods* make no one unclean, but the expression of the *heart*, in evil words and deeds, does. Mark saw the point and underlined it (Mark 7:19b). It took the church years to come to terms with it (see Acts 10–11 and Gal. 2).

TO THINK ABOUT: 'Attempt to reach righteousness by any way except that of Jesus and you will find out your mistake!' (Matthew Arnold)

A PRAYER: 'Create in me a clean heart, O God.' (Ps. 51:10)

15:21–28 A pagan woman's faith

For the second time we read of Jesus withdrawing from the public eye (compare 14:13), this time to the district of Tyre and Sidon, away from his own people. (Mark adds that he entered a house and wished no one to know it, Mark 7:24). It is likely that Jesus wished to be alone with his disciples; he will have been conscious of the limited time ahead of him and it was essential to prepare his men for their future tasks. But again, 'he could not be hid' (Mark 7:24). A woman from that area cried after him for help for her daughter. Matthew calls her a Canaanite, emphasising her non-Jewish race. The parallels between this narrative and that of the centurion who sought Jesus's help are striking (see Matt. 8:5–13): both were pagans; both sought help for one they loved; both met with resistance from Jesus (that is, if 8:7 is read as a query, see notes); both recognised their position as outsiders, without resentment; both manifested an outstanding faith; both were told that their request was granted, which involved a healing from a distance and itself required faith to believe; both found on departing that their loved one had been healed by Jesus.

Some have been puzzled by the way Jesus treated the woman, first by his silence on her initial request, and then by his apparent rebuff to her (26). It is essential, however, to take seriously something that the Gentile churches have tended to minimise: Israel was the covenant people of God, chosen to receive the revelation of God and to be the instrument of his salvation in the world; Jesus was sent *to them* in fulfillment of God's promise to raise up the Messiah among them, to enable them to rise to their calling of being the servant nation under the servant-Messiah, and to be the light of the world (so Isaiah 40–55). Jesus was not to be deflected from this task. It is nevertheless clear that he did respond to Gentiles who came to him in faith. The statement of v. 26 is less harsh than it may appear: Jews regarded the pariah dogs that roamed wild as the lowest form of animal, but house dogs were pets; they were allowed in the house to eat bread on which fingers were wiped at a meal. Jesus affirms that it is wrong to give bread prepared for children to the dog in the house; the woman replied, 'True, but pets feed on the bread which the children let fall!' The answer was as apposite as that of the centurion, and the faith it manifested was rewarded in a similar way.

TO THINK ABOUT: 'Faith in the promises and the accomplishment of the promises are inseparable. He that believeth shall enjoy' (John Owen).

15:29–39 More healings and feedings

Matthew's summary of the healing ministry of Jesus at this time (29–31) replaces Mark's account of the healing of one who was deaf (Greek, *kophos*) and dumb (*mogilalos*). Both terms are used in Isaiah 35:5–6, the latter very unusual (literally 'speaking with difficulty'). Matthew includes them both in v. 30, along with others in Isaiah 35, so underscoring the aspect of Jesus's ministry as the fulfilment of the promise of God's kingdom in Isaiah 35. The glorifying of 'the God of Israel' (31) is particularly appropriate after the healing of the Canaanite woman (21–28).

The relation of the feeding miracle in 32–38 to that of the five thousand has been widely discussed. Frequently it is urged that the later account is a variant report of the former. The difficulty for many is not that Jesus could or would perform the same miracle twice, but that the disciples behaved on the second occasion as though the first had not happened. It is, of course, possible that the query of v. 33 is a recollection of what the disciples had said earlier. The differences perhaps should be more carefully taken into account: on the second occasion the people were with Jesus for three days – a kind of convocation during which the stock of food was exhausted; and, of course, the figures differ. From the time of Augustine this difference in figures has been seen as the clue to the problem: the feeding of the five thousand was Jesus's gift of the bread of life to the Jews and that of the four thousand the gift of the bread of life to the Gentiles (*five* is a characteristic number for Jews, *four* for Gentiles; *twelve* baskets taken up by *twelve* apostles representing *twelve* tribes of Israel, in contrast to *seven* baskets, corresponding to *seven* Hellenist deacons (Acts 6) and the *seventy* nations of the world). In view of the nature of Jesus's dealings with Gentiles, illustrated in the previous paragraph (15:21–28), I think it wholly unlikely that Jesus fed a multitude of *Gentiles* in this way; but it is quite feasible that the evangelists saw in the second feeding miracle an anticipation of the Lord giving the bread of life to the nations *after the resurrection*. (A similar issue arises from the relation of the mission of the twelve, Luke 9, to that of the seventy, Luke 10; the latter was certainly a further mission to *Israelite* towns, but Luke will have seen it as an anticipation of the later mission to the *nations*.)

TO THINK ABOUT: As the tree of life yields fruit for the nations and leaves for their healing (Rev. 22:2), so there is bread enough and to spare for the life of the whole wide world.

16:1–12 The leaven of the Pharisees and Sadducees

The opening paragraph (1–4), is an interesting example of Matthew's use of his sources. He has already reproduced the account of the demand for a sign from Jesus in 12:38–9, taken from the so-called 'Q' source, the teaching material which he and Luke have in common (compare Luke 11:16,29). Now, as he continues to follow Mark, he comes upon the same incident (Mark 8:11–12), and he repeats it, because it leads so well into the following paragraph (5–12). At the same time he inserts between vs. 1 and 4 another saying from 'Q', vs. (2–3), reproduced in Luke 12:54–6. This latter passage is very pertinent to Pharisees and Sadducees: they are able to read the signs of the sky regarding weather; why can they not read the signs of the times and see that their refusal of the word of God through Jesus will bring judgement from God and disaster from their Roman overlords?

The warning against the leaven of the Jewish leaders (6) and the conversation to which it leads is contained in all three synoptic Gospels, and the differences are significant (see Mark 8:14–21; Luke 12:1). The incident should be read in the light of Mark's observation (6:52) on the astonishment of the disciples at the stilling of the storm by Jesus: 'They did not understand about the loaves, but their hearts were hardened' (i.e. their minds were blinded). They should have recognised two things: (a) that God almighty works uniquely through Jesus; (b) that the miracle of the loaves was a revelation of God's continuing care for his people. The latter is clear in the famous saying of Deuteronomy 8:3 (so often misunderstood by us): 'He humbled you and let you hunger and fed you with manna . . . that he might make you know that man does not live by bread alone, but that *man lives by everything that proceeds out of the mouth of the Lord*', i.e. man can depend on the God who speaks the needful word of power that can meet our need. So the disciples should have realised that the leaven of which they must beware is that of the Jewish leaders. Luke speaks of it as hypocrisy (Luke 12:1), Matthew as teaching (12). It will be precisely the hypocrisy of their teaching which Jesus had in mind. For examples of the hypocrisy of the Pharisees' teaching, see 15:3–9; 23:16–32; for that of the Sadducees compare 21:12–46; 22:23–32, their disgraceful actions in the trial of Jesus, and bringing about his death.

TO THINK ABOUT: 'The corruption of the best is the worst.' There is nothing more damning than the use of religion as a cloak for godless living. Let us always seek reality and utmost sincerity in our profession of the faith of Christ.

16:13–20 The Christ and his church

There are not many passages in the Bible as concentrated as this one. We must try to do some concentrated thinking about it. The incident forms the watershed of the ministry of Jesus. To it he had led his disciples, from it he unfolds the nature of his mission and destiny – the cross and resurrection and the kingdom for the world.

The question of v. 13, so worded in Matthew alone, is an example of 'Son of man' for 'I', which we should render, 'Who do men say that *I am*?' Peter's answer in v. 16 must be understood in strictly Jewish terms: 'You are the Messiah, the king whom God has installed, the son who represents the son-of-God nation' (compare Ps. 2:7 and Exod. 4:22–3). The revelation of the unity of the Son with the Father had not yet been grasped by Peter or by any other disciple.

Jesus pronounces a blessing on his disciple: 'Blessed are you, *Simon*, son of John'. He is blessed because the Father himself has revealed to him the truth about the Messiah-son. This revelation is followed by another – from Jesus: 'And *I tell you*, you are *Kepha*, and on this *kepha* I will build my church'. 'Peter' is a Greek name which translates the name Jesus actually gave him (Paul uses it sometimes, see Gal. 2:11,14); we should translate, therefore, 'You are *Rock*, and on this *rock* I will build my church'. Had the Catholic tradition not read into this saying the extraordinary notion that Jesus has given a Peter in every subsequent generation to guide his church, none would have queried its natural meaning: Jesus was to build his church of the future, which was to replace the temple as the place where God would be met (compare Matt. 26:60f; John 2:19), on the foundation of *Peter confessing the revelation from the Father about the Son*. This use of the figure of the church as the temple of God built on the aspostolic witnesses to Christ appears in Ephesians 2:19–21, and in a different manner in Revelation 21:14. To Peter were given the 'keys of the kingdom of heaven'; not of the church, but keys to open the door of the kingdom of salvation through preaching Christ, its Lord and Saviour. He must 'bind' in their guilt those who reject the good news, but loose from their guilt those who receive it (the metaphor is from the law court, the pronouncement of sentence by a judge). At this juncture of the Lord's ministry the Jews cannot possibly understand all this; hence the injunction to silence in v. 20, lest great misunderstanding arise.

TO THINK ABOUT: As the people of the kingdom, the church is essentially the church of the resurrection, which the gates of death cannot hold in; the people of the new life, in this world and the next. *Let the world see it!*

16:21–28 The Christ and his cross

It is doubtful that the modern Christian can possibly enter, even imaginatively, into the shock which the disciples experienced when they heard Jesus saying, 'The Son of man . . . must suffer many things . . . and be killed' (13, 21). That repudiated everything that they had believed from childhood concerning the Messiah, and everything that they expected from Jesus. It was not at all mitigated by the reference to the resurrection, for to the disciples that would have indicated only that Jesus would share in the resurrection of the last day, admittedly not far off, but appallingly overshadowed by his death. Peter voices his reaction: 'This shall never happen to you!' And then he receives his second shock: Jesus addresses him as though he were the devil! He's acting as the mouthpiece of *Satan*, the *adversary*. The 'Rock' is shattered!

In reality v. 21 contains an extraordinary summary of Old Testament prophecy: Jesus as the Son of man of Daniel 7:13 (so Mark 8:31) is to fulfil all the intimations of the suffering of God's servants for the kingdom – the righteous who suffer at the hands of the godless, the rejected prophets, the martyrs who give their lives for God's truth and glory, and the Servant of the Lord who bears the sin of the many; all this comes to a head in him whose service is to bring to man God's saving sovereignty.

In accordance with this announcement a new note is struck for the disciples of Jesus: he calls them to join him in shouldering a cross and in sharing his destiny (24). Paradoxical as it appears, this is the way to real life, the life of the kingdom of God. All self-seeking in the light of this goal is self-destruction, and all true self-sacrifice is self-preservation (25). Not even the possession of the whole world can take the place of this gift of life (26). The day when the Son of man is revealed will make this plain (27). This the disciples will grasp shortly when they catch a glimpse of the glory of the Son of man in his kingdom (so Matthew would have us understand verse 28, compare 17:1–8).

A PRAYER: Lord, in the strength of grace, with a glad heart and free,
Myself, my residue of days, I consecrate to thee.

(C. Wesley)

Questions for further study and discussion on Matthew 14:22–16:28

1. What does 14:22–33 contribute to our understanding of Christ?

2. Are there traditions of the church which hinder the word of God? (Compare 15:4–9.)

3. What has 16:2–3 to teach us concerning 'signs of the times' in our day?

4. Reflect on the teaching of 16:17–19 as to the nature and task of the church.

5. Consider the meaning of 16:24 for the early Christians, and for us.

17:1–8 The Christ in his glory

The event inevitably calls to mind the baptism of Jesus, when the heavens opened, the Spirit descended and the Father's voice came to Jesus, expressing his delight in his Son (3:13–17). This occasion is explicitly described in v. 9 as a vision; a vision employs figures and images familiar to those who receive them.

Why did the vision occur at this point in the ministry? Without doubt because of the critical event that had just taken place in the confession of Jesus as Messiah and the disturbing teaching that Jesus then gave to his disciples. As Jesus had withdrawn his disciples from the public eye to teach them the secret of his mission, so he now takes his three closest associates to the solitude of Hermon, to commit himself to the Father for the journey that was to issue in his final sufferings and death (for a comparable withdrawal with the three, cf. Gethsemane, Matt. 26:36–46). The transfiguration experience was the Father's answer to the Son's surrender and prayer; he strengthened his Son for the task in view and, in the holy fellowship, gave an anticipation of the glory to which it would lead (compare 2 Cor. 3:18–4:1). The disciples were also drawn into the vision; for them it was a confirmation of their acknowledgement of Jesus as the Messiah ('This is my Son', v. 5) and, in particular, a confirmation that the path of Jesus through suffering to glory was according to the Father's will ('*Hear* him!'). The remarkable feature of this confirmation is its use of visionary elements associated with the coming of the kingdom of God which is the goal of Christ's work: *Jesus is glorified*, as he will appear in his final coming (note especially 2 Pet. 1:16 in this connection); *Moses and Elijah are with him*, not solely as representatives of law and prophets, but as those expected with the last days (compare the imagery of Rev. 11:3–12); *the cloud* that envelopes the Lord, the two prophets and the three disciples, is reminiscent of the cloud of glory in which the Lord is to be revealed (see Matt. 24:30); *the voice from heaven* is often mentioned in such visions of the end (e.g. Rev. 21:6); *the two prophets from the past* recall 'the dead in Christ', and *the three disciples in the present* 'those that are alive and are left' (1 Thess. 4:15). Thus the divine confirmation to the Son and to the disciples is a revelation of his glory in the kingdom for which he labours, manifested in his ministry, seen in his resurrection, to be unveiled in his coming.

TO THINK ABOUT: We bow before the heavenly voice
Which bids bewildered souls rejoice:
'Though love wax cold, and faith grow dim,
This is my Son: O hear ye him!'

(A. P. Stanley)

17:9–20 From mountain to valley

The conversation between Jesus and the three disciples in 9–12 is clearly determined by the experience they had just had. The command of Jesus to let no one know of what they had seen 'until the Son of man is raised from the dead' is comparable to other similar demands (see especially 16:20); but the disciples were perplexed by this reference to the 'resurrection from the dead' (Mark 9:10). The readers of the Gospel know that not till Easter can the Christ and his redemptive works be understood. The disciples, however, have witnessed the glory of Christ in his kingdom; yet the Bible teachers of their day, the scribes, say that Elijah must come before the kingdom; how can that be so? The scribes, of course, are echoing Malachi 4:5: Elijah is to come and restore the disrupted family order (contrast Mic. 7:6), lest the last day be judgement day for all ('lest I come and smite the land with a curse'). Jesus affirms the teachings: Elijah does come and restore all things (Septuagint wording), but he adds that Elijah has come already, and men got their way with him: what Jezebel failed to do, her successor achieved, and the new Elijah, John the Baptist, was killed. That, too, is what lies ahead for the Son of man (12).

From the heights of Hermon to the depths of appalling need: such was the descent of Jesus to the demoniac boy. His desperate sigh of v. 17 was not for the boy's father alone; Mark makes it plain that 'the perverse and crooked generation' of Moses's time (Deut. 32:5) was reproduced again in the scribes, the disciples, the father, the onlookers – indeed the whole generation to which they belonged (see Mark 9:14ff). None of them had 'faith as a grain of mustard seed' (20), or the boy would have been healed. After setting the boy free Jesus explained to his disciples: the tiniest element of the genuine article of faith can do the impossible ('moving mountains' was a proverbial expression for doing the apparently impossible), since it looks to God, for whom the moving of mountains is a small thing. This paradox of the smallest and the greatest emphasises that even for the weakest who truly trusts God, the resources of Almighty God are ready to go into action.

TO THINK ABOUT: 'The promises of God are apprehended by faith; hope cannot reach them; love cannot understand them; they surpass our longings and desires; they may be obtained, but cannot be estimated' (Augustine).

17:22–27 The Lord and the temple tax

For the second time Jesus makes an explicit statement concerning the fate that lies ahead of him, in language similar to that of 16:21. A significant difference is observable, however. We read that the Son of man is 'delivered up' into the hands of men. If we ask, Who is to deliver up the Son of man?, the Gospels supply various answers: *Judas* delivered up Jesus to the Jewish leaders (26:46–47); the *Jewish priests* delivered up Jesus to Pilate (27:2); and *Pilate* delivered up Jesus to the soldiers for crucifixion (27:26); the early church recognised that ultimately it was *God* who delivered up Jesus for our sins (e.g. Rom. 4:25). The thought is rooted in the final 'servant song', Isaiah 52:13–53:12. The term occurs in Isaiah 53:12, 'his soul was delivered up to death' (Septuagint); the equivalent Aramaic term appears in the Targum of Isaiah 53:5; and the thought is embodied in 53:10: 'It was the Lord's will to crush him and cause him to suffer . . . and make his life a guilt offering'.

The incident that follows, strange as it may seem to us, must have been of intense interest to Jewish Christians in the early church. Since all Jews were expected to pay an annual tax to the temple authorities, they naturally wanted to know whether Jesus had said anything about it. For the question of Jesus in v. 25 it is important to recognise, (a) that the tax was rooted in the law (Exod. 30:13) and therefore was not merely traditional; (b) that Jesus assumes the eastern custom of levying taxes on foreigners as tribute, not on the subjects themselves; since Jesus and his disciples stand to God as 'sons', he the mediator of the kingdom and they its true subjects, he and his followers should be exempt from the tax (the rest of the Jews should pay, since they were 'aliens'!). Nevertheless, to avoid offence, Jesus authorised Peter to pay the tax for them both. On the means whereby the money was to be found, a comment of Schlatter is pertinent: 'The silver piece brought from the fish should be set alongside the donkey in Bethphage and the upper room in Jerusalem, all of which were ready for Jesus. In all three narratives Jesus receives what he needs from the Father, through whom his poverty is to be transformed in the consummated kingdom'. Accordingly, what Jesus needs, God makes available, so that his mission can be fulfilled.

AN ASSURANCE: No strength of our own or goodness we claim;
Yet, since we have known the Saviour's great name,
In this our strong tower for safety we hide –
The Lord is our power, the Lord will provide.

(J. Newton)

18:1–14 Jesus and the little ones

There is an ambiguity in this passage as to the identity of the 'little ones'. Clearly vs. 3–4 speak of children, as also v. 5. The same may apply to v. 6, but the expression, 'little ones who believe in me', could include the despised and humble believers among Jesus's followers; the like applies to v. 10, and yet more so to v. 14 since Luke adduces the parable of the lost sheep among those parables that relate to Jesus associating with the outcasts of society. These sayings express the concern and care of Jesus for those who are reckoned to be of no importance; they are important to God, and therefore to him.

In v. 1 Matthew has abbreviated Mark's account of the question as to the greatest in the kingdom, possibly not only because of length, but because it sets the disciples in a poor light (Mark 9:33–37). Jesus calls a child, sets him in their midst, and makes two statements: (1) Unless men 'turn and become like children' they will have no part in the kingdom, let alone be great in it. This is paraphrased by Jeremias as, 'learning to say "Abba" again, putting one's whole trust in the heavenly Father, returning to the Father's house and the Father's arms'. (2) The one who is humble as a child is greatest in the kingdom. How ashamed the disciples must have been at these words!

It is equally astonishing that Jesus linked himself so completely with a child as he does in v. 5, where the sin of causing 'little ones who believe in me' to stumble evokes the strongest expression of judgement. This leads to further sayings on the things that cause stumbling from God's way: they must all be renounced (see Matt. 5:29–30). Verse 10 expresses God's care for the 'little ones' who, whether children or adults, appear to believe (cf. 'these little ones', in 10 and 14). Floyd Filson comments on the saying: 'That these angels have direct access to God ("see his face") means that God always knows the plight of his little ones, cares for them, and will vindicate them if they are despised or ill-treated'. The like concern of God is mirrored in the parable of 12–13; it relates primarily to God as Shepherd, not Jesus, and consciously echoes Ezekiel 34 (especially 7–16). Its pertinence to Jesus is that he acts as his Father does – he seeks that which is lost, because all such are precious to God.

A PRAYER: 'O Lord, I fling myself with all my weakness and misery into thy ever-open arms. Pour the life-giving balm of thy love into my heart. Do for me what I have not the courage to do for myself. May I be thine, wholly thine, and at all costs thine' (Pere Besson).

18:15–22 Fellowship and discipline

This passage, like 10:5ff and 23:2f, is indicative of the strongly Jewish background of Matthew's Gospel. The situation in view in 15–18 is of members of a synagogue obedient to the word of Jesus ('church' here simply means 'assembly'). There were no churches in the days of our Lord's ministry. The passage tells how fellowship and discipline should be maintained according to God's law. The meaning of v. 15 is uncertain, since the terms 'against you' are omitted from some of our best and earliest manuscripts and by some of the best informed early Christian writers. If the words are omitted the principle applies to a brother who has committed a wrong, not who has wronged a brother. In either case the situation calls for private entreaty; 'you have gained your brother' is illuminated by James 5:19–20. Refusal to listen to an individual should be followed by action according to Deuteronomy 19:15. If the brother still will not listen, the congregation is to be told; if he refuses to heed even the community he is to be regarded 'as a Gentile', hence not of Israel and 'as a publican', and so not of the congregation. Here the principle of 16:19 holds good (18): the brother is either declared to be guilty ('bound'), and is to be excluded from the congregation (until his repentance, of course); or he is acquitted ('loosed'), presumably on his public acknowledgement of his fault.

The passage has been preserved by the Jewish churches after Pentecost and reproduced by Matthew, because they saw it as authoritative teaching of Jesus for his followers. To it, Matthew has added the encouragement to prayer in v. 19, which is applicable among followers of Jesus at any time and in any place. Verse 20, however, though reflecting Jewish thought ('Where two sit and the words of the Law are between them, the Shekinah rests between them'), is applicable only to the period of the church after Easter; it comes from the end of the ministry of Jesus when his death and his resurrection are anticipated, and is one with the promises of the Lord's presence given in the upper room discourses (for example, John 14:18–24; 16:16–24).

The answer of Jesus to Peter appears to be a conscious adaptation of Genesis 4:24, where Lamech claims a right to return harm 'seventy-sevenfold' on any who harms him (the Septuagint renders, seventy-times seven); The unlimited revenge of primitive man is to give place to unlimited forgiveness on the part of Christ's followers.

TO THINK ABOUT: 'Where Christ is, there is the church'. Jesus applies that truth for the lowest limits of fellowship: two believers, together in his name!

18:23–35 A parable of forgiveness

The limitless forgiveness of v. 22 receives a marvellous illustration in the parable before us. A man is depicted as owing a debt unimaginably great – he must be understood as a minister of state responsible for the finances of the kingdom. The size of his debt should not be translated into modern currency values. Jeremias pointed out that the figure combines the highest number available to the ancients with the greatest currency unit known. Such a debt could never have been paid by any individual, no matter how many wives and children and possessions he had to sell. Precisely because of his utter helplessness the king listened to his pleas, and remitted the entire debt. Infinite indebtedness was met with infinite compassion. But the freed debtor walked out of the king's audience chamber and met a fellow servant who owed him a sum which, to a man in his position, was trifling. He demanded instant payment of the debt and refused the plea which he himself had just made of the king – time to pay. He handed the man over to the torturers till the debt was paid. The contrast in behaviour was shocking and it brought the wrath of the king on the head of the unforgiving man.

The lesson of the parable is clear. None can be indebted to us as we have been indebted to God; we are called on to forgive as we have been forgiven. D. Via sums up the close of the parable thus: 'To receive (18:32) without giving (18:33) is self-destructive (18:34)'. Observe, however, that this is not merely a law of existence, it is the *principle* of God's kingdom, hence the warning of judgement that is added (35). Nevertheless the emphasis of the parable is positive – a call to live according to the grace bestowed by the Lord in his saving kingdom. He who opens his life to that grace will act in the spirit of the Lord.

TO THINK ABOUT: 'If mercy by its nature has the character of an ordinance, it cannot be an exception, but only the norm' (Eta Linneman).

19:1–12 Marriage and divorce

The brief statement of our Lord's teaching on divorce given in 5:31–32 is more fully stated here in a discussion with the Pharisees. In response to their question, which takes up the language of Deuteronomy 24:1, Jesus calls attention to the creation narratives. God made man 'male and female' (Gen. 1:27), and this unity of man the creature comes to its completest expression when man and woman become 'one flesh' (Gen. 2:24). Since this was God's intention in creating man, a husband should not put asunder what God himself joined (note, it is the *husband* who is addressed here, not the lawyer!). The Pharisees counter by asking why Moses *commanded* a man to give a bill of divorce and put his wife away. The passage does not say that. Jesus rightly saw that Deuteronomy 24:1–4 tells what a man may not do *if* he does divorce his wife and she remarries; there is no command to divorce; in our Lord's mind this entails, rather, a concession, necessitated through the hardness of man due to his falling away from God's purpose. The so-called 'exceptive clause' in v. 9, while not in Mark, is in the spirit of Jesus's teaching; but note again, there is no demand from him that divorce *must* then take place, contrary to the rabbis, who ruled that it should.

Verses 11–12 are often separated from the former paragraph in the conviction that Jesus takes up the observation of the disciples in v. 10 with a qualified approval, as though to say, 'Celibacy all round is desirable, but celibacy all round is impossible; let those who can, do it' (T. W. Manson). This appears to me doubtful. Matthew surely intends us to relate v. 11 to the Lord's teaching in 5–6: this high rule of marriage may indeed be beyond the ability of many. But where life is ruled by the maxim, 'for the sake of the kingdom of God', men will be able to fulfil God's intention in marriage, just as other men for the sake of the kingdom of God will be given grace to renounce marriage.

A PRAYER: (Be specific – pray either for your own marriage, or adapt the prayer to ask for the strengthening of someone else's.) Grant us to be of one heart and of one mind, united in love to you and to each other in you, and in our joint service of your kingdom.

Questions for further study and discussion on Matthew 17:1– 19:12

1. What does John 1:14 suggest as to the significance of the transfiguration?

2. Consider the meaning of 17:20 for the life of faith today.

3. What can we learn from 18:2–14 regarding a child's relation to God?

4. Discuss the theme of discipline in the church in the light of 18:15–18.

5. What has 18:23–35 to say to unforgiving *Christians*?

19:13–22 Children, wealth and the kingdom of God

This passage presents to us two famous incidents, both highly compressed by Matthew. They supply a lesson in contrasts on who belongs to the kingdom of God.

It was customary for Jewish children to be brought to rabbis to be blessed, especially on the day of atonement, though there is no indication in our text that the incident in v. 13 took place on that day. Doubtless the disciples felt that Jesus should not be troubled in this way; he was no ordinary rabbi and he had more than enough to do. The saying of Jesus in v. 14 is frequently generalised, as though it affirms that the kingdom of God belongs to all children everywhere. Others interpret the phrase, 'such as these', as denoting people of a child-like spirit, not children as such. We should interpret the passage in its context. It is *children brought to Jesus* who are said to be heirs of the kingdom (compare the language of 5:3). These are its heirs because they manifest a childlike attitude to the Bearer of the kingdom (observe how Mark interprets this saying, Mark 10:15; Matthew has used that idea in 18:3 and so omits it here). The Catholic exegete, M. J. Lagrange, puts it beautifully: 'To receive the kingdom is to receive Christ, the gospel, grace. In a word the reign of God is an invitation, a call. Children respond at once to a call from people they know, and they run and throw themselves into their arms. Those who will have responded will enter into the kingdom'.

The narrative of the wealthy questioner is calculated to astonish in a Jewish setting, where wealth was a sign of God's favour. The man's desire is to possess 'eternal life', that is, life in God's kingdom when it comes. Matthew eases the question of Jesus in v. 17, in order to avoid misunderstanding (see Mark 10:18). On the claim of the man to have fulfilled the latter half of the ten commandments, which relate to the command to love one's neighbour (see 22:34–39), Jesus tells him what to do if he would be 'perfect', that is, if he would show neighbour love of the divine sort (compare 5:48): he bids him give his wealth away and join his company. The first sentence was so shocking that the second was not heard. He turned from him who asked so much, and in so doing spurned the unspeakable privilege of living in the company of the one who bestows the life of the kingdom of God. Clinging to this world he threw away the life he sought, life now and hereafter.

TO THANK GOD FOR: How vast the treasure we possess!
How rich thy bounty, King of grace!
This world is ours, and worlds to come,
Earth is our lodge, and heaven our home.
(Isaac Watts)

19:23–30 The great reversal

Through the intervening years the church has been as hesitant as the original disciples to accept the plain meaning of 23–24. We have been anxious to tone down the unpalatable language – in part so as not to put off other attractive rich young men from joining the church. So we suggest that the needle's eye is a low gate in Jerusalem, through which camels go with difficulty, or that 'camel' here represents a sailor's word for a rope. The explanation about the camel's gate, still shown in Jerusalem, is an invention of tourist guides for the gullible and goes back to the early part of this century. The Jews of Jesus's day used similar proverbial language, only substituting 'elephant' for 'camel' (making the task a trifle more difficult!). Jesus is stating baldly a transparent fact: that money militates against consecration to the service of God and cross-bearing after Jesus. But let us as readily acknowledge that most of us in western civilisation are wealthy in comparison with Jesus and his apostles, and far more so when compared with one third of today's world. The challenge of 23–24 must be accepted by us all: it's difficult for people like us to get into the kingdom of God.

Jesus went further. The astonished disciples, hearing that the favoured of God will have a hard time entering the kingdom of God, asked, 'Who then can get the life of the kingdom ('be saved')?' His reply was, 'Nobody – unless the God who can do the impossible gives it'. We must understand v. 27 as uttered with a splutter: the outraged Peter asks what God will do for them who have forsaken everything for the kingdom. The answer is in two parts. Mark and Luke make v. 29 the immediate reply to the question: Everyone who has sacrificed for the kingdom of God ('for my name's sake') will receive a hundred-fold – in this life (Mark 10:30) – and in the coming age will receive *as a gift* eternal life, that is, the salvation which is impossible for man to earn. Secondly, in the inauguration of the new world, when the Son of man sits on his throne to determine who will enter it (see 25:31, where language identical to 28 is used), the apostles who proclaimed the kingdom to Israel will sit with him in Israel's judgement. As the representatives of the Son of man in proclaiming the kingdom to Israel, they will be witnesses to Israel's response to the proclamation. In that day the great reversal will take place, according to God's estimate of man (30).

(Note: *never* in the New Testament does 'judge' mean 'rule'. The thought of v. 28 is rooted in Daniel 7:18 and is applied by Paul to the church in 1 Cor. 6:2.)

TO THINK ABOUT: What are the implications of Romans 8:15–17, especially 17b?

20:1–16 The labourers in the vineyard

The parable follows the saying of 19:30 and ends with a repetition of it. Matthew will have wished us to see that, in contrast to the rich young ruler and all he represents, 'the last to be called are the first to taste the sovereign goodness of the Master' (P. Bonnard). In the context of our Lord's ministry the 'last' are the publicans and sinners who respond to the call of Jesus, while the 'first' include those who object to his association with such.

The details of the parable are easily understandable, but the story it tells shocks modern susceptibilities, accustomed to Trade Union demands for adequate compensation for work done. Two factors in the background help to explain it. First is the dire unemployment in Palestine in the time of Jesus. It brought poverty and hunger without relief. Jeremias suggests that it is out of pity for their poverty that the owner of the vineyard is depicted as paying a full day's wages to men who had not earned it; the action is not arbitrary, but motivated by compassion for the poor (compare v. 15). Secondly, Jesus had become notorious for his association with the 'last', i.e. with people regarded by the 'first' as the dregs of society, religiously as well as socially. To claim, as Jesus did, that the kingdom of God belonged to such appeared to the Pharisees and all like-minded Jews as outrageous; they denied that such people had any part in the kingdom and affirmed that he who preached otherwise was teaching contrary to the law of God. The parable sets forth a different view: that God is compassionate as well as holy. Out of his heart of grace he gives, to those who have no claim on the kingdom, full entrance into it. As Jesus earlier justified his going to the lost, by depicting God as the Good Shepherd (18:12–14), so here he cites the Father's compassion on the undeserving as the motive for his own concern for them. Those who object to the Son are objecting to the Father. There is an unspoken warning here that the 'last' had better think again, lest they deny themselves of that which they would deny others. The 'righteous' need conversion as well as 'sinners'!

A PRAYER: 'Thine are goodness, grace, love, kindness, O thou Lover of men! gentleness, tenderness, forbearance, long-suffering, manifold mercies, great mercies, abundant tender compassions. Glory be to thee, O Lord' (Lancelot Andrewes).

20:17–34 Precedence in the kingdom of God

For the third time Jesus warns the disciples of what lies ahead in Jerusalem (17–19). If the earlier warnings had not sunk into their minds, neither did this one (see Luke 18:34). On the contrary, it is evident that as the journey to Jerusalem progressed the excitement of the disciples mounted. Luke records a parable of Jesus, told 'because they supposed that the kingdom of God was to appear immediately' (Luke 19:11). Presumably it was this anticipation that motived the request of the sons of Zebedee, through their mother, to be seated at either side of Jesus in his kingdom (20–21). The response of Jesus is in line with everything that he had taught about the coming of the kingdom: it comes through sacrifice – through drinking a 'cup' of suffering and (in Mark 10:39) through a 'baptism' in waters that destroy; accordingly, leadership in the kingdom assumes leadership in the suffering by which the kingdom comes. To the credit of James and John they declared that they were ready to drink the cup (and endure his baptism), and Jesus affirmed that this they would do. (They did, but in different ways; compare Acts 12:2 with the long life of John in the service of Christ.)

The indignation of the other disciples was countered by Jesus with a fresh application of the lesson given in 18:4: leadership in the kingdom of God is not patterned after that of this world's rulers, but on self-abnegating service, the pattern of which is the service of the Son of man, which is to reach its climax in the yielding of his life as a ransom for many (25–28). As has been observed: 'Jesus' death was the last consequence of his ministering self-giving; in this death the real dimension of Jesus' action on sinners during his ministry was revealed' (Roloff). The 'ransom for many' was the means of a new exodus for humanity, a deliverance from slavery to sin and death into life in the kingdom of God; through it the kingdom was to be opened for every child of man.

Such a Saviour, on his way to that sacrifice, readily listened to the pleas of the blind for sight (29–34). Receiving it, they 'followed him' – all unwittingly to the city which kills prophets and stones those sent to her (23:37). The Jerusalem road means different things for different people (sometimes the City listens! – see Acts 2:43–47; 5:12–16; 21:20). The Saviour's disciples must be ready, and willing, for anything.

A PRAYER: Thou hast said in season, 'As is the master shall the servant be';
Let me not subtly slide into the treason,
Seeking an honour which they gave not thee.

(F. W. H. Myers)

21:1–11 The entry into Jerusalem

Was the entry of Jesus into Jerusalem a purely spontaneous event, or was it a kind of manifesto planned by Jesus? Matthew shapes his report to make two points clear: (1) the event was in accord with the declared purpose of God, (2) it was in accord with the intention of Jesus. It was Jesus who took the initiative in sending two disciples to Bethphage to fetch a donkey. Had he arranged with its owner to lend the beast? Possibly, but consider Wellhausen's comment: 'We must not rationalise here. Jesus has not already ordered the colt, nor made an arrangement with its owners, but he knows beforehand what will happen, because God who directs what is to happen is with him'. Matthew speaks of *two* beasts, an ass 'and a colt with her'. He is often charged with misunderstanding Hebrew parallelism, since Zechariah 9:9 has one beast in mind, not two (compare the citation of the passage in John 12:15), but the Jewish evangelist can hardly have been so ignorant of biblical language and poetry as that. He is underscoring two features, the fulfilment of Zechariah's prophecy, cited in v. 5, and the immaturity of the colt on which Jesus rode, which could not leave its mother (an ass with foal is a common sight in Palestine to this day).

The waving of palm branches (8) symbolised a victorious welcome. Their use at the feast of tabernacles may have inspired the cry 'Hosanna' ('save now!') from Psalm 118:25, and the blessing from Psalm 118:26, which should read, 'Blessed in the name of the Lord is *He who comes*' – i.e. the Messiah! This is not diminished by the saying of v. 11, 'This is the prophet'. Jesus is the prophet of the last times – the one like Moses (Deut. 18:15), powerful to save!

Jesus was not taken by surprise in this event. He inspired it. For the first time in his ministry he steps into the open and manifests who he is: the Messiah, Son of David, yes, but not a warrior like David; he is the prince of peace, of whom the scriptures say, 'Behold your king comes!' (Zech 9:9), and 'Behold, your salvation comes!' (Isa. 62:11).

TO THINK ABOUT: O lowly majesty, lofty in lowliness!
Blest Saviour, who am I to share thy
blessedness?
Yet thou hast called me, even me,
Servant divine, to follow thee.
(G. W. Briggs)

21:12–17 The cleansing of the temple

Again we have a well known event in the life of Jesus clarified for us by the Old Testament citations which it contains. In v. 13 two quotations from the prophets are made by our Lord. The first is from Isaiah 56:7, 'My house shall be called a house of prayer for all peoples'. Both Matthew and Luke omit the last phrase ('for all peoples'), probably because they wrote after the temple had been destroyed, but the phrase is important because of the context of the oracle (see Isa. 56:3–8) and because the temple trade was carried out in the only place where representatives of the nations could come – the 'court of the Gentiles'. The second scripture, briefly alluded to in v. 13, comes from Jeremiah's discourse against the temple: 'Has this house, which is called by my name, become a den of robbers in your eyes? Behold, I myself have seen it, says the Lord . . . I will do to the house which is called by my name, and in which you trust, and to the place which I gave to you and to your fathers, as I did to Shiloh', i.e. God will bring a destructive judgement upon both temple and people (Jer. 7:11–15). Whereas the Jews of our Lord's time looked for the Messiah to renew the temple and its worship, Jesus by deed and word shows that it is to be done in a more drastic manner than they had imagined (see Matt. 23:38; 24:2; 26: 60–61). 'The cleansing of the temple becomes simultaneously a judgement and an expression of hope in a better fellowship than that based on the temple as it was' (B. Gärtner).

The healings within the temple courts emphasise the messianic significance of the event. Blind and crippled people were forbidden by Pharisees to enter the temple courts, hence their double offence at what Jesus was doing and at the cries of the children. Matthew will have derived satisfaction from Jesus's citation of Psalm 8:3; it continues (in the Septuagint): 'Out of the mouth of infants and sucklings you have perfected praise *because of your enemies, to destroy the enemy and the avenger*'. The Pharisees were well and truly rebuked!

'The ministry of Jesus means judgement, whether he comes to Jerusalem or into our own lives, which consent to so much that is contrary to his will and harbour sentiments and practices to which he is irrevocably opposed. Those who have not encountered the fire of his righteousness, which is inseparable from redemptive activity, have not yet entered his presence' (Harold Roberts).

21:18–22 The withered fig tree

Mark presents this story in two stages, enclosing his account of the cleansing of the temple (Mark 11:12–14, 20–25), a significant pointer to the interpretation of the event. He further states the astonishment of the disciples at the condition of the tree on *the following day*; Matthew's 'at once' is due to compression, but is correct comparatively – the withering took place speedily.

The fig tree in Palestine is very early with its leaves, but its ripe fruit does not come till June. With the leaves, however, green knops appear, and if there are none of them the tree bears no figs that year. Lagrange, who spent a lifetime in Jerusalem, pointed out that these early fruits are hardly edible, though children do sometimes eat them. We must take it, nevertheless, that since Jesus was hungry he went to the tree to stave off his hunger with them (19a); since the tree had leaves, it should have had the green fruit. When he saw that it had none he determined on an act of prophetic symbolism. Frequently in the Old Testament Israel is described as a tree without fruit, but Micah 7:1 is so pertinent to this passage it may well have been in our Lord's mind: 'Woe is me! For I have become as when the summer fruit has been gathered, as when the vintage has been gleaned: *there is no cluster to eat, no first-ripe fig which my soul desires*', whereupon a day of judgement is announced (Mic. 7:4). The tree before Jesus was like the nation, making profession of godliness but without the reality – least of all in Jerusalem, with its magnificent temple and corrupt priesthood and teachers of the law who professed much but yielded little for God (Matt. 23:3–7). Accordingly, a word of judgement from Jesus that strikes down the profitless fig-tree, affords a parable of the judgement which is to fall on the city, temple and nation.

The event is seen as a lesson on faith: faith can move mountains, and receive answers to prayer (21–22).

TO THINK ABOUT:
> Who the line shall draw, the limits of the power define,
> That even imperfect faith to man affords?
>
> **(Wordsworth)**

Questions for further study and discussion on Matthew 19:13–21:22

1. How can 19:13–15 be embodied in the life of the church?

2. How should we apply the lessons of 19:16–30 to ourselves and to others today?

3. Construct an exposition of 20:1–16 to a factory shop-steward.

4. What were the fundamental misconceptions regarding the nature of the kingdom of God and the life of its members, that led the mother of James and John to ask her question (20:20–28)?

5. Why did the two blind men call Jesus 'Son of David'?

6. Suggest parallels to the cleansing of the temple in the experience of the church.

21:23–32 Challenge to the authority of Jesus

So far in the Gospel story those who have opposed Jesus have been Pharisees and scribes (most of whom belonged to the former group). Now the chief priests and elders confront Jesus, and that for a clear reason: they were in charge of the Jerusalem temple, and the ejection by Jesus of the traders from the temple courts was an affront to their authority. They therefore ask Jesus: What sort of authority do you have, and who gave it to you? The counter question of Jesus in v. 24 is presumably linked with their question. Its key terms are, 'from heaven' and 'from men': was John authorised *by God* to proclaim his message and administer his baptism of repentance, or was his ministry based on his own assumption of authority? The pertinence of the question was evident, since it was known that the ministries of John and Jesus were linked; Jesus had publicly affirmed that John's ministry was 'from heaven' (11:7–15) and John had likewise borne testimony to Jesus, above all as recorded in John 1:19–34 which denotes Jesus as the leader of God's flock, who was to deliver his people and rule them in the messianic age. If John's ministry was 'from heaven', then it is plain that that of Jesus had the same origin. The Jewish leaders knew themselves to be 'on the spot'. In their embarrassment they could only declare their ignorance (25–27).

The parable that follows (28–32) is an exposure of the challengers of Jesus. The two sons are clearly identifiable: the one who refused to work in the vineyard but repented and, later, went into it represents the 'sinners', those outwardly disobedient to the law of God but who have now repented and are doing God's will; the son who professed obedience but by his action proved disobedient represents the Jewish leaders. So Jesus declares to the latter: 'The tax-collectors and the harlots go into the kingdom of God before you'. The shock and outrage of those men are better imagined than stated. The 'before you' implies 'They are on the way *and you are not*'. It is a strong call for repentance.

TO THINK ABOUT: 'It is the intention of God to be visible to those who seek him with all their hearts, and concealed from those who are disposed to shun him' (Pascal).

21:33–46 Parable of the wicked farmers

The opening of the parable is so similar to that of Isaiah's song of the vineyard (Isa. 5:1–7) that it would hardly be possible for Jewish hearers not to recognise it: the parable has in view Israel under God. The sending of servants to receive fruit from the tenants of the vineyard is also a clear representation of the sending of prophets, who were badly treated by the nation (Jewish teachers tended to increase rather than diminish the number of those so treated, compare 23:29–30). Whereas to the Christian the sending of the son of the vineyard owner seems a clear representation of the Christ who is Jesus, that identification would not be plain to the Jewish leaders. C. H. Dodd pointed out that the situation depicted in the parable had a very contemporary ring about it. Foreigners living abroad possessed large tracts of the country and let out their estates to Palestinians. It was bitterly resented by the nationalist Palestinians, and resentment was fostered by the Zealots. The assumption of the tenants that by killing the heir they can take possession of the property is similarly realistic: they assume that the owner is dead and that the son has come to claim his property; by the law of that time ownerless property belonged to the first claimants, so the tenants on the spot could naturally make first claim. The lawless behaviour of the tenants could well have reminded the Jewish leaders of the Zealotic groups of their day, so when they are questioned as to what the owner of the vineyard will do to the violent murderers of the son, they answer in a manner that condemns themselves (40–41), just as David did when questioned by Nathan in the celebrated parable of the rich man who wronged a poor man (2 Sam. 12:1–14). Our Lord then cites Psalm 118:22 and declares: 'The kingdom of God will be taken away from *you* and given to a nation producing the fruits of it'. The leaders have forfeited their claim to the kingdom; it will be given to those who receive the gospel of the kingdom brought by Jesus, who build on the stone rejected by the builders, and who constitute an 'Israel made new in the remnant' (F. C. Burkitt).

The priests and Pharisees were helpless in their anger (45–46). How tragic that they did not act like David and repent!

TO THINK ABOUT: Caiaphas had his justification for the death of the Son: 'It is expedient that one man should die for the people, and that the whole nation should not perish' (John 11:50). Pray that Israel's leaders and people may grasp the truth of Caiaphas's words better than Caiaphas did.

22:1–14 The parable of the marriage feast

The first section of the parable (1–10) is closely related to that of the great feast in Luke 14:16–24, but the latter section (11–14) has no parallel in Luke's parable. It is possible that Matthew has conjoined two parables, a version of Luke's known to him and another about a feast arranged by a king for his son's wedding, and that features of the latter were incorporated into the former (note especially the introduction and the murderous activity of the invited and their punishment by the king, 5–6, which remind us of the parable of the wicked farmers in 21:33–41).

Two features in the parable call for notice. The first is the proclamation, 'Everything is ready; come to the marriage feast' (4). The second is that those originally invited spurned the call, and the newly invited guests are streaming into the house and taking places at the tables which the original guests should have occupied. The parable appears to portray not the feast of the kingdom in the world to come, but a feast of the kingdom now spread, which some are enjoying and others through their folly are missing.

The latter section of the parable combines this thought of present grace and imminent loss. The guests are packed into the dining hall, and the king comes in to see them all. That was a joyous moment for all present – except for one: he had no wedding garment on, and when questioned by the king about it he had no excuse to make. The garment is almost certainly not one specially made for a wedding, nor one provided by the host, but simply a *clean* one. (Rabbi Johanan ben Zakkai told of a king who issued invitations to a banquet without stating the hour; the wise attired themselves, but the foolish went on with their work; when the call to the feast was issued, only those dressed in clean clothes were admitted.) In the parable of Jesus the unready guest is thrown into the outer darkness. The call to wear the garment of repentance is clear. The day of salvation is *now*! (2 Cor. 6:1–2).

TO THINK ABOUT: 'The King commanded to go out and take Ignorance, and bind him hand and foot, and have him away. Then they took him up, and carried him through the air to the door that I saw on the side of the hill, and put him in there. Then I saw that there was a way to hell, even from the gates of heaven, as well as from the city of Destruction' (John Bunyan).

22:15–22 Taxes for Caesar

The approach to Jesus of Pharisees and Herodians (supporters of King Herod) is the first of a series of attempts to discredit Jesus before the Jerusalem crowds and, potentially, the most explosive one.

The Romans imposed on provinces under their rule a head-tax for all men over fourteen years and all women over twelve, to the age of sixty-five. The tax had to be paid in silver coins issued by the emperor. The coin in question had on one side the head of Tiberius wearing a laural wreath, a sign of his divinity, and the inscription, 'Tiberius Caesar, majestic son of the majestic God'. On the other side were the words, '*Pontifex maximus*', 'Most High Priest', and a picture of the emperor's mother, representing Rome, sitting on a throne of the gods, with a sceptre in her right hand and an olive branch in her left, representing the peace of the gods. To the Jews it was downright idolatrous. Moverover it was a clear symbol of the power of Rome and its claim to sovereignty over them. The rabbis expounded the promise to Abraham, 'I will make thee a great nation', as meaning that Abraham's coinage will be current in all the world, i.e. that he will have universal dominion; the coins will have on one side the figures of Abraham and Sarah and on the other Isaac and Rebekah. So the atmosphere in the temple was electric when Jesus was asked the question of v. 17: to affirm the obligation to pay the tax would have identified Jesus as a quisling, to deny it would have provided evidence to accuse him of incitement to revolution. The dictum of Jesus, 'Give back to Caesar what belongs to Caesar' was more literally applicable than it would be in our society; all acknowledged that Caesar's coins were his property, so none could fault Jesus's command. And 'Pay back to God what belongs to God' was every man's bounden duty. The important point was that *neither demand affected the other*. The implications were, of course, wider, including obedience to Caesar when he asked only what was his; on that basis Paul expounded Christian citizenship in Romans ch. 13. John, in the book of Revelation, wrote what a Christian must do when Caesar asks for what belongs to God.

TO THINK ABOUT: 'The state has a defined task from God in this age. This both grounds its dignity and limits it. The state belongs to the form of this world which passes away. Christians, the people of the new world, are free alike in their subordination to and in their recognition of the state. Their citizenship is in heaven (Phil 3:20)' (Paul Althaus).

22:23–33 Sadducees and the resurrection

It is not easy to determine precisely the beliefs of the Sadducees, since Jewish descriptions of them come only from people hostile to them. Contrary to some popular ideas about them, they were conservative in their religious views and regarded the Pharisees' preoccupation with eschatological doctrines as 'modern'. While, like most Jews, they viewed the Old Testament as the law, expanded and explained in the rest of the books, they rejected the Pharisees' oral traditions about the law, and regarded doctrines not in the written law as without authority.

The rationale of the question addressed to Jesus about the resurrection is based on the notions of resurrection popularly maintained. In the Sibylline Oracles it is stated, 'God himself shall fashion again the bones and ashes of men, and shall raise up mortals once more *as they were before*'. That this would be to a resumption of physical relations was taken for granted, and in Enoch ch. 10 we have a very crude anticipation of men begetting thousands of children in the kingdom of God (hardly a woman's idea of heaven!). The trick question put to Jesus cites the so-called Levirate law of Deuteronomy 25:5–6, relating to two brothers living in the same extended family; if one dies without leaving a son, the surviving brother must take the widow of his deceased brother so that children should be raised in the name of the deceased; by this means the name of the latter is perpetuated and the family inheritance continued. The conundrum as to what happens in the resurrection when seven brothers have taken successively one woman as wife is intended to show that because such an absurd situation could never have been in the mind of the law-maker, the resurrection could not have been anticipated. Jesus countered this with two fundamental propositions: (1) the resurrection is not a resumption of existence like the present, but one befitting the new creation, with relations on an angel-like plane. (2) This hope of resurrection is inherent in the revelation of God in the scriptures, as Exodus 3:6 shows: God as the God of Abraham, Isaac and Jacob maintains them in the fellowship they had in their earthly pilgrimage, and so *keeps them for the day of resurrection into the kingdom of glory*. He is *the God of the living*!

TO THINK ABOUT: 'Where, and with whom, God speaks, be it in wrath or in grace, the same is immortal'. (Martin Luther). 'If there were no Creator, we would fall into nothing in death. But because God is, we fall into the arms of God' (Karl Heim).

22:34–46 The law and the Messiah

Mark calls the questioner about 'the great commandment' a scribe, Matthew a lawyer. He was an interpreter of the law and would know well that the legitimacy of the question was a matter of dispute. Israel Abrahams, a professor of rabbinic literature and deeply interested in the Gospels, pointed out that Jewish teachers discussed whether it was permissible to distinguish between 'light' and 'heavy' commands, i.e. between lesser and greater. Some denied it, since all the commands are of God and therefore all of equal value; two questions are therefore involved: Did Jesus think it right to single out a 'great commandment'? If so, which one? The reply of Jesus is unambiguous: it *is* legitimate to fasten on first principles in the law, but it is not one command but two. The first came as no surprise to his hearers, for they had all recited it that morning; it is from the 'Shema' ('Hear O Israel . . .'), Deuteronomy 6:4, which had to be recited daily by every Jew. The second was less frequently on their lips: 'You shall love your neighbour as yourself' (Lev. 19:18). Other Jews may have conjoined these two commands. The *Testaments of the Twelve Patriarchs* three times repeats the dictum, 'Love the Lord and your neighbour', but since the work has been interpolated by a Christian editor we are uncertain whether these too are from a Christian. In Luke 10:25–27 a 'lawyer' actually gives this answer, but when Jesus agrees with him he is defensive, and asks who his neighbour is; this arises because in Leviticus ch. 19 'neighbour' means 'fellow Jew', and Pharisees would have allowed it only to Jews who kept the law. For Jesus, however, the law and the prophets 'hang' on these two commands, and they are at the root of his teaching. Love for God and love for neighbour are inseparable; without the latter the Shema is recited in vain.

The question put by Jesus to the Pharisees in 42–46 is a challenge, not to the Messiah's descent from David, but to viewing the Messiah primarily as *Son* of David, hence owing his position to his descent from David. On the contrary, David in Psalm 110 acknowledges him as *the Lord at God's right hand*. That had not been faced by the Pharisees. Christians know that the Messiah is *both* Son of man and Son of God. They embrace the whole teaching of the scriptures concerning their Lord!

A PRAYER: 'O blessed Lord, who hast commanded us to love one another, grant us grace that, having received thine undeserved bounty, we may love everyone in thee and for thee' (Anselm).

23:1–12 Warnings against the Pharisees

In the discourse before us we have an expansion of Mark's brief paragraph, Mark 12:38–40, with other sayings of Jesus relating to the scribes and Pharisees. 23:1–12 extends Mark's vs. 38–39; 23:13–36 extends Mark's v. 40, and 37–39 complete it with the lament over Jerusalem, found also in Luke 13:34–35.

The most surprising element in this chapter is the positive way in which it begins. Jesus says, 'The scribes and Pharisees sit on Moses's seat' (a long stone seat from which the teaching was given in the synagogues); they present themselves as authenticated exponents of Moses's teachings, and Jesus does not dispute it. On the contrary, so long as they do not smother the word of God with tradition, he tells his disciples to 'practice and observe whatever they tell you'. The prime objection of Jesus to the Pharisees was not their exposition of the scriptures but their lack of obedience to them: 'they preach, but they do not practise'. A perusal of the criticisms given in 13–32 bears this out; they are an exposure of hypocritical behaviour. 'Jesus's opposition concerned that which made man *man*, not that which made him a thinker and a talker' (A. Schlatter).

The Pharisaic emphasis on the externals of religion is illustrated in their making 'their phylacteries broad and their fringes long' (5). Phylacteries were leather or parchment cases containing Exodus 13:1–10, 11–16; Deuteronomy 6:4–9; 11:13–21, and which were worn on the head and forearm (see Deut. 6:8). The 'fringes' were tassels on garments, in accordance with Numbers 15:38; Deuteronomy 22:12. The prohibition against titles in 8–10 relate to honorific terms. 'Rabbi' literally means 'my master'; 'Father' was used in address to rabbis and older men; 'teacher', Greek *kathegetes*, was a superior term (in modern Greek, *professor*), and was applied in the Qumran sect to their authority, the Teacher of Righteousness. These titles are needless, since all are brothers and sisters, one is Father, and Christ is the supreme interpreter of the divine revelation.

A PRAYER: 'O Lord, give us all grace, by constant obedience, to offer up our wills and hearts an acceptable sacrifice unto Thee' (Christina Rossetti).

Questions for further study and discussion on Matthew 21:23–23:12

1. Give a *Christian* answer to the question posed in 21:23.

2. What application has 22:1–14 to professed Christians?

3. Discuss the Christian's political responsibilities in the light of 22:21.

4. Has the parable of 21:28–32 anything to teach us about our tendency to ignore certain groups or classes within our society, assuming that they will reject the claims of Christ? In the light of this parable, can you think of a way of making your church's evangelistic activities more relevant?

5. How is 22:29 possible for one who tries to live according to the rules of the Bible?

6. How can you put the twin *commands* to love (22:37–39) into practice, today?

7. What temptations might compare with those of the Pharisees in 23:5–10, which are faced by church leaders today?

23:13–28 Woes on scribes and Pharisees

Some writers have urged that the woes in 13–33 are unduly severe on the Pharisees, since much Pharisaic writing is nobler than the representations of them here. The latter observation is true, yet vs. 13–33 are one with the picture of the Pharisees elsewhere in the Gospels, and we recall their part in securing the death of Jesus. At this time there must have been a debasing element in Pharisaism, out of harmony with its beginnings among the Hasidim and with the later rabbinic developments, and which would have been condemned by both.

The first of the seven woes of this chapter (13) entails the imagery of the key which opens the doors of the kingdom of God (see Luke 11:52; Matt. 16:19). The scribes possess the key that can open the kingdom to men and women, through their knowledge of the scriptures which point to Christ; but they misuse them in their opposition to the representative of the kingdom. Their blindness to the fulfilment of God's word in Jesus leads them to refuse to enter themselves and to direct people away from the Christ. This is a heinous sin.

Missionary work was not strong in Jewish tradition – they thought in terms of the nations being attracted to Judaism rather than the Jews going to them (compare Isa. 2:2–3; Zech. 8:20–23). The Pharisees took up the task enthusiastically, with grim results (15). Their verbal jugglery in the oaths which were binding and those which were not (16–22) throws light on Jesus's opposition to oaths in 5:33–37.

The enthusiasm of the Pharisees for the minutiae of the law is seen in their scrupulous application of Leviticus 27:30 (23); Jesus does not condemn this, but he does denounce the scrupulosity which can have such concern but overlooks the cardinal prophetic principles of Micah 6:8. This is certainly 'straining out a gnat and swallowing a camel'! Zeal for the external is again illustrated in the simile of washing the exterior of cups and dishes; the Pharisees should be concerned about their interior life more, and about external appearances less.

The tombs mentioned in v. 27 were whitewashed to draw attention to their presence, so that people could avoid contracting defilement through indirect contact with the dead. But the whitened tombs are symbols of the living dead!

A PRAYER: Above the swamps of subterfuge and shame,
The deeds, the thoughts, that honour may not name,
The halting tongue that dares not tell the whole,
O Lord of truth, lift every Christian soul.

(H. M. Butler)

23:29–39 Inexorable judgement

In 29–32 there is an allusion to a 'renaissance of tomb-building' (Jeremias) that took place in the era of Jesus. Beginning with the building of a monument at David's tomb by Herod the Great, these memorials to the prophets and righteous men served both to honour the dead and expiate the guilt of slaying them. Jesus protested that the builders of the tombs were proving to be the 'sons' of the guilty in more than one sense: they were sons who inherited their fathers' characters by rejecting God's anointed one and seeking to kill him. By so doing they will 'fill up the measure of their fathers' and bring on themselves God's wrath (32).

Luke's version of 34–36 is prefaced with the words, 'the Wisdom of God said' (Luke 11:49). It is likely to embody a citation from an existing wisdom-saying, in which wisdom sends its messengers to God's people in vain. Jesus sees his own mission as the climax to the experience of God's representatives, so the blood of the righteous from the beginning of the Old Testament (Genesis) to its end (2 Chronicles in the Hebrew Bible) will be demanded of 'this generation' (note: 'Zechariah, son of Barachiah' is a copyist's slip (see Zech. 1:1) for 'Zechariah, son of Jehoiada', 2 Chron. 24:20–22; Matthew would not have been guilty of a confusion of that order).

The lament over Jerusalem (37–39) reflects the many visits of Jesus to the city, such as are mentioned in the Gospel of John, and the continuous resistance of its people – 'you would not'. The lament therefore leads to judgement: 'your house is forsaken' (38). The 'house' most plausibly refers to the temple, rather than to the city; its abandonment by God leads to its eventual destruction (see the process illustrated in Ezek. 9:5–6; 10:4–5, 18–19; 11:22–23). When the house of God becomes empty of God it loses its significance in God's sight.

But the prophecy of judgement ends on a note of hope: the day will come when Jerusalem will welcome its returning Lord with the ancient cry of Psalm 118:26: 'Blessed be he who enters in the name of the Lord'. In the triumph of Christ the sinful people repents of its guilty rejection and will be given, with believers of all nations, a place among the heirs of the kingdom which the Christ had died and risen to open for all.

A PRAYER:
O come, O come, thou Lord of might, who to thy tribes on Sinai's height
In ancient times didst give the law, in cloud and majesty and awe.
Rejoice! Rejoice! Immanuel
Shall come to thee, O Israel!

24:1–14 The temple and the end

The last of Matthew's discourses, chs. 24–25, is concerned with the impending judgements to fall on Israel, and with our Lord's coming in glory. It is important to recognise that, as with the other discourses in Matthew, this one consists of sayings brought together from varied occasions: **1–36** = Mark 13:1–32; **37–40** = Luke 17:26–7, 34–5; **42–51** = Luke 12:42–6. Moreover, Mark ch. 13 itself has been formed through a similar process. There are four chief themes in the chapter: (1) the tribulation of Israel, 1–2, 15–22; (2) the tribulation of the followers of Jesus, 9–14; (3) the appearance of false Christs and of the true Christ, 5, 23–27, 29–31; (4) Christ's coming and watchfulness (32, 37–51).

The discourse sets out from our Lord's prediction of the ruin of the temple, v. 2. Did the disciples call his attention to its stupendous buildings (1) because of his earlier statements about the temple and city (e.g. 23:38; Luke 19:44)? Jesus is yet more emphatic: not one stone shall be left on another! The broken relationship with God brings a rejection of the place which serves as a visible embodiment of God's presence with his people.

The question of the disciples in v. 3 is inevitable: every Jew assumed that *that* temple would be the centre of the earth in the kingdom of God; its ruin then could only be in connection with the end of the age and the coming of the final kingdom. Hence the first word of Jesus's reply is, 'Take heed' (4). The whole intent of the discourse is summed up in this word; it is not information for the curious,but exhortation to be ready.

Observe the stress on the 'not yet' of v. 6 and 'this is but the beginning of the sufferings' in v. 8; in other words, 'always beware of date-fixers!' And they must be ready for suffering, 9–13, for Christ's representatives have to bear his reproach – 'for my name's sake' (9). Their great responsibility is to see that the gospel of the kingdom is preached throughout the world (14); for the Christ is to die for the whole world, and people can know it only if those who know tell them.

TO THINK ABOUT: 'No stone of the house can know another destiny than that meted out to the Christ as the corner- and foundation-stone. What the Christ as the primary element of the Church suffers, the Church nowhere and never can be spared' (G. Gloege).

24:15–28 The sign of 'the desolating sacrilege'

The disciples had asked the time and sign of events surrounding the ruin of the temple (4); v. 15 gives one regarding the temple, v. 30 another regarding the coming of Christ. The 'desolating sacrilege' of v. 15 ('abomination of desolation', AV) is mentioned in Daniel 9:27, 11:31, 12:11 and reflects a word-play: instead of 'Lord of Heaven' (*Baal-shamaim*), 'Desolating Sacrilege' (*Shiqqutz Shomem*) was substituted. It originally referred to a heathen altar, placed on the great altar in the temple by Antiochus Epiphanes, with an image of Zeus ('Lord of Heaven') made in his own likeness; it was crowning attempt to force Israel to become a pagan nation. The expression became a type of antigod rebellion in the world. On the lips of Jesus it denotes a horrifying desolation of the temple (and city? see Dan. 9:26), reminiscent in some way of that of Antiochus, in all probability through the pagan forces of Rome (compare Luke 21:20). When that happens the Jews should 'flee to the mountains' (compare Gen. 19:17; Jerusalem is another Sodom!). For these are days of 'great tribulation' (21). The same situation is in mind as that from which Jesus started in v. 2: verse 15 employs Daniel 9:27 to explain its nature, and now Daniel 12:1 is used for the same purpose; it denotes Israel's judgement as *the day of the Lord on the city and nation*, just as the prophets had spoken of the day of the Lord on cities and nations in their days.

The warnings against false prophets and false Christs in 23–26 are given in the light of the Jewish belief that the Messiah grows up in secret and will be made manifest at the right time (through Elijah's anointing of him, said some rabbis); this made possible constant false claims about alleged messiahs. On the contrary, said Jesus, when the Messiah comes, all will know; he will come with the suddenness, the visibility and the universality of lightning (27). So, also, as surely as vultures appear where carrion lies, disaster will fall on Israel swiftly, suddenly and with unerring judgement (28).

TO THINK ABOUT: 'Set the trumpet to your lips, for a vulture is over the house of the Lord, because they have broken my covenant, and transgressed my law' (Hos. 8:1). 'My heart's desire and prayer to God for them is that they may be saved' (Rom. 10:1).

24:29–36 The sign of the Son of man

The observation earlier made that the discourse consists of material brought together from varied contexts applies especially to this section. The sayings have been preserved and grouped by teachers in the churches prior to the evangelists (for another example of this procedure compare Luke 16:14–15, 16, 17, 18, independent sayings handed on without context).

The description of the confusion in the universe in v. 29 takes up prophetic language about 'theophany', the coming of God in judgement and salvation (compare Isa. 13:10, 34:4; Joel 2:10, 3:15–16). There is no thought in such passages of the break-up of the universe; they give poetic pictures of the terror of the universe before the almighty creator as he steps forth to judge and save (for an instructive example of these images see Hab. 3:3–15). Their significance in this context is the representation of Christ's coming in terms of a theophany; it is beyond all powers of description, but has the nature of a divine intervention.

Matthew alone mentions the sign of the Son of man (30). It adapts the figure of the 'standard' or ensign which God sets up for the rallying of his dispersed people (Isa. 11:12); the thought is continued in the mention of the trumpet in 31, compare Isaiah 17:13. The sign of the Son of man most plausibly signifies the (*Shekinah*) glory with which he comes for the redemption of his people. Then he will 'gather' them, in Mark's language, 'from the ends of the earth to the ends of heaven', i.e. universe-wide. The fig tree parable (32–33) bids the disciples to see in their trials and tribulations the pledge of the kingdom of God; it conveys assurance of the coming of resurrection life into this 'wintry' age.

The closest parallel to v. 34, and that which provides its true reference, is 23:36: 'all this will come upon this generation', namely the judgement described in 23:32,35, corresponding to 15–21 in this chapter. By contrast, v. 36 clearly relates to the time of Christ's coming ('that day' and 'that hour' are synonymous); the time is known alone to the Father because he alone determines it; unlike some of his followers, the Son is content to have it so (see Acts 1:6–7).

TO THINK ABOUT: Surely he cometh, and a thousand voices
                  Shout to the saints, and to the deaf are dumb!
                  Surely he cometh, and the earth rejoices,
                  Glad in his coming who hath sworn, 'I come'.
                                    (F. W. H. Myers)

24:37–51 Alertness in view of the end

Our passage follows v. 36 well: in view of the unknowable time of the coming of Christ it is necessary to be constantly on the alert.

The coming of the Son of man is compared to the days of Noah (and Lot, in Luke 17:26–30). Contrary to expectations, the comparison with the flood generation is not to underscore the extremity of wickedness, but to highlight the dangers of preoccupation with everyday occupations (38). Two thoughts appear to be in view. The first: *unreflective absorption* in the common things of life on the part of people who have no thought for God, and so live as though there were no death, or even in spite of the reality of death ('Let us eat, drink and be merry, for tomorrow we die'). The other is the *unexpectedness* of the end for all such.

A similar point is made in the comparisons of 40–41 (compare Luke 17:34–35). Three pictures are given, of two men working in a field, two women grinding meal, two people sharing a bed; Matthew and Luke each give two, having the second only in common. These illustrate the separation which the Lord's coming will bring about, dividing men and women bound by closest ties on earth. In each case one is 'taken' and the other 'left'; the former are 'taken' to be with the Son of man in his Father's kingdom. The command is given, 'Watch therefore, for you do not know on what day your Lord is coming' (42). This does not mean to gaze in the sky all day long (Acts 1:11), but to live in a state of spiritual alertness, ready at any hour for the Lord.

Two parables illustrate the point: the 'thief in the night' (43–44) could have been inspired by an actual burglary that had set people talking; it illustrates the necessity for preparedness for an *unexpected* coming, which could bring disaster instead of blessing (compare 1 Thess. 5:2; 2 Pet. 3:10; Rev. 3:3, 16:15). The parable of the faithful and unfaithful servants (45–51) illustrates that watchfulness includes being occupied in faithful discharge of responsibilities committed to one; the drunk and faithless servant is like the man surprised by the burglar: he loses all (50–51).

TO THINK ABOUT:
Ye servants of the Lord, each in his office wait,
Observant of his heavenly word, and watchful at his gate.
O happy servant he, in such a posture found;
He shall his Lord with rapture see, and be with honour crowned.

(P. Doddridge).

25:1–13 The wise and foolish maidens

The kingdom of heaven is likened to ten girls and a wedding. They were probably servants, whose task was to meet the bridegroom as he came to take his bride to the marriage ceremony. That the bridegroom should come at midnight is foreign to western ways, but not to the middle east. Here a typical wedding is described: 'Having amused oneself with dancing and other entertainments, one starts the wedding feast by nightfall. By torchlight, songs and exultation, the bride, attended by women, is later led from her parents' house to her new home, where she is entertained by her companions. Suddenly, usually around midnight, it is announced that the bridegroom comes. The women then leave the bride alone and go with torches to meet the bridegroom, who approaches at the head of his friends' (L. Bauer). The time of the groom's arrival is unpredictable and usually delayed, for a simple reason: he has to bargain with the bride's family about the dowry he pays for her! The necessity of the girls to be ready with their lamps, then, is plain: the lamps must be burning while the groom is awaited and extra oil is needed in view of his possible delay. There is no mystic meaning in the oil, as though it represented the Holy Spirit. Lamps won't burn without it! The wise girls took an extra supply, the foolish didn't. When the cry went out, 'Behold, the bridegroom!' (6) the latter said, with dismay, 'Our lamps are going out!' (8). The wise refused to give their oil, since their lamps could have gone out too, and the bridegroom would have had no lights. So the foolish girls missed the wedding.

The lesson is simple: 'Watch, for you know neither the day nor the hour' (13).

TO THINK ABOUT: 'Watch . . . means in the time of "night" to stand with burning lamps, prepared to receive the coming Bridegroom, to be "awake" in the life of salvation (in Christ), and, concentrated on and awaiting the return of the Son of Man, to live in preparedness for this' (E. Lovestamm).

Questions for further study and discussion on Matthew 23:13–25:13

1. Does oath-making have religious implications? Is it ever legitimate to swear an oath? (23:16–22)

2. What does 23:23 suggest about the practice of tithing?

3. How does the Christian mission relate to the coming of Christ (24:14)?

4. What can we learn about signs and the end from 24:32–36?

5. With the coming of Christ in view, what practical hints on how to live now can you find in chapters 24 and 25?

25:14–30 The parable of the talents

The parable of the talents and that of the pounds in Luke 19:11–27 portray an essentially similar situation, though diverging in many particulars. The situation in Matthew is determined by the huge sums of money entrusted by the master to his servants; v. 14 indicates that it was his whole capital, 'his property'. In the ancient world wealthy men often deposited their money with traders for profit; Hammurabi drew up laws concerning transactions of this sort in Babylonia. The man in the parable took a risk in handing his money to his men, but he trusted them. The sums differed according to their capabilities, but the 'one talent man' still had a tremendous responsibility given him.

Two servants responded well to the trust reposed in them. The third did nothing, beyond hiding the talent in the earth for safety (had he died it would have been lost!). On his return the master held a reckoning with his servants. The 'five talents man' and the 'two talents man' received identical commendation from their master (21,23), since both showed faithfulness according to their ability. The third excused his indolence by accusing his master of rapacity, and to his accusation added insolence (24–25). The master's reply pointed to a simple recourse to which he could have gone, namely put the money to bankers and so gain interest (Jeremias suggests that that was precisely what the others did: the enormous rates of interest doubled the invested money!). The talent entrusted to the slothful man was taken from him and given to the worthiest servant.

To what reality does the parable point? To the Pharisees, whose self-righteousness was of no use to God? To the scribes, to whom the treasure of the word of God was entrusted? The parable of the treasure in the field would suggest rather that the talents represent the kingdom of God, offered as a gift to men, which becomes a powerful agency in their lives. If so, the parable shows that the call into the kingdom demands response and responsible service. The third man represents those who are hearers of the word but not doers (Jas. 1:22–25). At the master's return the 'doers' enter into his joy, they participate in the delights of the feast of the kingdom; the hearer who did nothing about the call is thrust into the darkness outside, gnashing his teeth at what he is missing (30). We who have received the offer of the kingdom should check to see how positive our response is.

TO THINK ABOUT: 'Jesus does not allow his servants to live only for themselves, and misinterpret their position merely as their own transference into life. The parable establishes that *wherever the gift of Jesus is received, the purpose of life extends beyond one's own ego*' (A. Schlatter).

25:31–46 The sheep and the goats

This much discussed and preached on passage is not an ordinary parable, for its parabolic elements strictly extend only to 32–33. Nor is it an apocalyptic vision of the judgement in the ordinary sense, for its central interest lies in the dialogue of 35–40, 42–45. There are parallels to the framework of the judgement scene in apocalyptic literature, notably in the *Similitudes of Enoch*, as there are parallels to the dialogue in Jewish ethical literature, yet there is no parallel to the parabolic vision as a unity. The unique feature of the passage is the relation of the King, who is Son of man, to those he calls 'the least of these my brethren' (40,45), for it is response to this relationship that is evaluated in the dialogue and in virtue of this the judgement is pronounced.

Who are these 'least' to whom the deeds of 35–40 are done? Not Jews over against the Gentile world, nor Christians over against the non-Christian world. The scene in the vision assumes the resurrection of the dead, hence *all* humanity stands before the King – Jews, Gentiles, professing Christians, heathen, the lot. Astonishingly, the Son of man professes his unity with mankind in *all* places and times. Deeds of love and compassion shown to individuals are accepted as done to him, even as those withheld from individuals are viewed as withheld from him. These deeds are so valued because they are works of God, and the Son was sent to do such works in his own life and death for mankind. For those who confess faith in his name, the reality of their confession is tested to the extent they walked in his ways; for those who never knew him, the expression of the same mercy is tested and accepted, or its absence rebuked. Most remarkable of all, the solidarity of the Son of man with mankind in his birth, his baptism, his ministry, his death and his resurrection is confessed by him in the judgement. In him, the mediator of redemption and of judgement, the divine mercy is revealed in its glory at the end.

'At the Last Judgement the heathen will be examined concerning the acts of love which they have shown to me in the form of the afflicted, and they will be granted the grace of a share in the kingdom, if they have fulfilled Messiah's law, the duty of love. Thus for them justification is available on the ground of love, since *for them also the ransom has been paid* (Mark 10:45)' (J. Jeremias).

26:1–16 Conspiracy and devotion

It is generally agreed that the events leading to the arrest, trial and crucifixion of Jesus were the first Gospel narratives to be brought into a continuous account, since people needed to know how it came about that the Messiah was put to death through the leaders of the nation and the Roman authority. Each evangelist presents the story with particular needs in mind. Matthew lays emphasis on the sinfulness of the Jews in rejecting Jesus, and the establishment of the church as the new Israel, but emphasises above all the majesty of Jesus as he proceeds to his coronation via his cross. He is not victim but master of his destiny.

This last point is hinted at in v. 2: the Lord announces his handing over to death *before* the sanhedrin meets to determine how to do it (3). In the early account the offer of Judas to betray Jesus at a price (14–16) probably followed at once. Into this context of conspiracy and treachery the story of a woman's sacrificial devotion to Jesus was inserted (6–13), making a striking contrast to the actions of the Sanhedrin and Judas.

We have no information concerning Simon the leper (6); some guess that he was the late husband of Martha, since she is said to have owned the house in which she and Mary lived (Luke 10:38). We know from John 12:1ff that the woman was Mary, Martha's sister. The costliness of the ointment used (9) is stressed in Mark (Mark 14:5), a working man's wages for a year! Why did she do it? The answer depends on how Jesus's words in v. 12 are understood. Did he interpret generously a simple act of devotion by Mary, beyond her knowledge? Or did he know that she had divined more than his disciples? One clue is in Mark's statement that Mary broke the flask containing the ointment (Mark 14:3); in that period it was usual to break the flask after anointing a dead body and to put it in the coffin. By this act she may have shown to Jesus her understanding of what lay ahead of him and so she anointed him as *the king who is to die*. So interprets A. M. Hunter: 'Her act said more plainly than words to Christ, "I know you are the Messiah, and I know that a cross awaits you". It was this insight that moved the Lord to such splendid praise'. The recording of this act in the Gospel ensured, beyond the evangelists' knowing, the fulfilment of the promise in v. 13.

A PRAYER: 'Lord, do thou turn me all into love, and all my love into obedience, and let my obedience be without interruption; and then I hope thou wilt accept such a return as I can make' (Jeremy Taylor).

26:17–30 The Last Supper

Matthew has abbreviated Mark's account of the arrangement with an unnamed man to take over his 'upper room' for his last meal with the disciples (Mark 14:12–16). It was the *passover* meal that was being celebrated (17). In John's Gospel it is crystal clear that Jesus died as God's passover lamb, at the time when the passover lambs were being slain for the passover meal (see John 19:14; and compare v. 36 with Exod. 12:46). It appears that Jesus with many Jews of his day, including the Qumran covenanters, celebrated passover on Wednesday and not according to the date fixed by the temple authorities.

At the meal Jesus told his disciples that one of them was to betray him (20–25). The heinousness of the act is indicated in v. 22: it is one who actually dips his hand with Jesus in the dish! (Compare Ps. 41:9. Lawrence of Arabia, when a wanted man with a price on his head, could always reveal his identity to Arabs after he had eaten bread with them: in Eastern etiquette one never betrays a man with whom one shares a meal.)

The account of the meal in 26–29 is compressed, reflecting its use in the Christian observance of the *Lord's* Supper (as 1 Cor. 11:23–26). In the meal the bread was shared at the beginning; the cup ('of blessing', 1 Cor. 10:16) at the end. Jesus relates both to himself, making them a double parable of his sacrifice. The broken bread represents his 'body' – his total self: 'He interprets *himself* as the source of blessing and salvation, as Mediator of salvation' (R. Pesch). The wine represents his blood, but in a complex manner: v. 28 echoes Exodus 24:8, Jeremiah 31:31, and Isaiah 53:12. Through the blood of Jesus God brings about a new covenant to bring into existence a new Israel, i.e. a new people of God, cleansed and renewed by the Spirit, for life in his eternal kingdom. The reference to drinking the cup in the kingdom of God (29) is not intended to give a date, but to show the goal of God's redemptive work through Jesus. Every celebration of the Lord's Supper is intended to be an anticipation of the fulfilment of the passover in the feast of the kingdom of God. Had the disciples understood, they would have sung the second half of the Hallel psalms (Psalms 114–118) with joy as well as tears. It requires eyes opened through the resurrection to do that.

TO THINK ABOUT (carefully!): 'It is the Last Supper which makes Calvary sacrificial' (A. E. J. Rawlinson).

26:31–46 Gethsemane

On the way to the Mount of Olives Jesus made known to the disciples that they were about to desert him, in fulfilment of Zechariah 13:7. It must have seemed to them impossible, hence the outburst of Peter (33, echoed in John 21:15) and the yet more shocking prediction of his denial in v. 34. Viewing the scene from our detached viewpoint, Jesus's language is deeply significant: it shows that he saw his followers as the true flock of God, of which the Old Testament spoke, and that he was the Shepherd who must lay down his life for the sheep: this relation he will sustain after the resurrection – 'I will go before you to Galilee' (32). C. H. Turner commented on this: 'As he had "gone before them" in the days of his awe and consternation (Mark 10:32) from Galilee to Jerusalem, so in the days of his victory he would "go before them" from Jerusalem to Galilee'.

The company arrives at Gethsemane ('Olive press'), on the western side of the Mount of Olives. Jesus takes his three closest disciples, that they may support him in sympathy and prayer in his distress; sadly, they were incapable of sharing with him in this darkest hour of his life. They failed to 'watch and pray' even for themselves, with the result that they did 'fall into temptation' (41) when the crisis came upon them. But why was Jesus so deeply 'sorrowful and troubled' (37)? Not primarily through the failure of his mission to Israel, nor through natural shrinking from death, but rather by reason of the nature of the ordeal facing him. His prayer in v. 39 indicates this: 'If it be possible *let this cup pass from me*'. The terrifying thing about the coming ordeal was that it meant taking a cup from the hands of God and, in biblical imagery, that constantly denoted experiencing the wrath of God (see, for example, Isa. 51:17,21–23; Jer. 25.15–29; Ezek. 23:31–34, and compare Luke 12:49–50). Jesus faced in Gethsemane the full consequences of enduring judgement for man and the onslaught from the powers of evil (Luke 22:53); it brought the kind of desolation of spirit that wrung from him on the cross the cry of desolation (Matt. 27:46). From this he shrank; but for this he had come; he therefore wrestled in prayer, till he could affirm with all his heart what first he prayed in weakness: 'Thy will be done'. The battle was won before it was joined – in the garden.

FOR REFLECTION: Ah, thou who sorrowest unto death,
We conquer in thy mortal fray;
And earth for all her children saith,
'O God, take not this cup away!'
(James Martineau)

26:47–56 The betrayal and arrest of Jesus

Judas arrives on the scene with an unexpectedly large crowd, armed with swords and clubs (47). From John 18:3,12 we learn that Roman troops from the Antonia garrison had joined the forces mustered by the Sanhedrin. It was this to which Jesus objected in v. 55: the authorities were acting as though he were an armed bandit, a dangerous insurgent requiring armed troops to restrain him. This procedure of the authorities falls into line with their charge against Jesus, that he claimed to be a 'king', an upstart revolutionary against the government (Luke 23:2). Since Judas knew that they would find Jesus in a garden, dark with trees, he had arranged a sign by which he would identify Jesus: he would greet him with a kiss (48). In itself this was nothing exceptional, since a kiss was the normal way for a pupil to greet his rabbi. But Matthew and Mark uses the same terms for the agreement and the act: 'The one I shall kiss (*phileso*) is the man' (48); 'and he gave him an affectionate kiss' (*katephilesen*). Xenophon observed the distinction when he spoke about *kissing* the good man, but *tenderly kissing* the kind. (See further, Luke 7:38,45; 15:20; Acts 20:37). This led George Herbert to put on the lips of Jesus the words:

> Judas, dost thou betray me with a kiss?
> Canst thou find hell about my lips, and miss
> Of life, just at the gates of life and bliss?

An attempt of a disciple to defend his master with his sword is instantly stayed by Jesus (51). None of the synoptic Gospels discloses who he was, probably for reasons of prudence; John, writing at a later date, tells us that it was Peter (John 18:10). But Jesus is still master of the situation: he declines equally the use of weapons (52) and to appeal to his Father for the aid of angelic forces (53). If the latter sounds strange to us it was not so to Jesus's contemporaries. The Qumran community regarded themselves as one with the angelic host in heaven and anticipated fighting along with them in the last battles against the armies of wickedness in the world. Jesus, standing in the midst of such forces of evil, is calm: 'All this has taken place that the scriptures . . . might be fulfilled' (56). The Lord who gave the word to the prophets is in control.

TO THINK ABOUT: 'The way of the cross is not a sad second choice, but is God's way to achieve his purpose' (Floyd Filson).

26:57–68 Jesus before the sanhedrin

In recent years an idea has been gaining support that the passage before us is historically untrustworthy. It is urged that it has arisen from a desire to fasten the blame for the death of Jesus on the Jews, whereas Jesus was *crucified* by Romans, after trial by *Pilate*; had Jesus been found guilty by Jews he would have been stoned (it is argued, on the basis that John 8:31 is incorrect, that they could have done this). This view is being taken up by Jews the world over, who are charging Christians with falsifying history in making them responsible for the death of Jesus. It has been closely investigated by Christian scholars. The British jurist A. N. Sherwin-White has shown that the trial narratives of the Gospels agree exactly with criminal procedures in provinces of the Roman empire and that John 18:31 is correct: Romans did not allow subordinate governments to carry out executions, least of all by those hostile to Rome; the Jews had to formulate a charge against Jesus and take it to the Roman governor, as the Gospels state.

The evidence for such a charge was nearly found in the saying of v. 61; assault on the temple was an offence in the eyes of the Roman authorities, but the saying was too slippery to lay hold of (compare John 2:19). The high priest then tried his hand: putting Jesus on oath before God he demanded to know whether he was the Messiah (63). Jesus affirmed that he was, but not as Caiaphas understood the term ('*You* have said so.' v. 64): Caiaphas and his court will see him as the Son of man, seated at God's right hand and coming with the clouds of heaven (64, citing Ps. 110:1 and Dan. 7:13). They are to see him, not *at* Easter, but as the Lord raised at Easter to God's right hand, when he comes in power and glory. 'Hereafter', more strictly 'from now on', conveys the sense: 'From this hour on, since you utter judgement, you will experience the Son of man only in glory and prepared for judgement over you' (W. Trilling). The high priest tore his robes at the 'blasphemy' (65); his action was suitable for one who must acknowledge his appalling error in the day of our Lord's coming with power to reign.

TO THINK ABOUT: Isaiah 52:15.

Questions for further study and discussion on Matthew 25:14–26:68

1. If 'talents' represent the kingdom of God, how does one trade with them?

2. How does 25:31–46 affect our witness to (1) non-Christians, (2) Christians?

3. Consider the significance of 26:11 for the Christian's use of his resources.

4. What is the connection between the Lord's Supper and the kingdom of God?

5. What may we learn from 26:39 concerning our prayers?

6. What areas of life are there where we are unwilling, either as individuals or as a church, to identify ourselves totally with Christ (compare Peter's response, 26:58)?

26:69–75 Peter's denial of Jesus

It is ironical that no incident in Peter's life is so well known as this one. In mitigation we must acknowledge that he put himself in a dangerous situation when he entered the high priest's courtyard; he could have been recognised – and he was (John 18:26) – but he could not tear himself away from his Lord in that terrible hour.

From John we learn that the first girl to address Peter was responsible for letting people in and out of the courtyard. She let him in at the request of the 'other disciple' who was an acquaintance of the high priest (John 18:15–17); Mark tells that she stared intently at Peter before saying anything (Mark 14:67). Peter moved away from the fire and went into the forecourt to escape unwelcome attention, but in vain: the bystanders were told, 'This man was with Jesus of Nazareth' (71). The oath which accompanied his denial was not 'bad language', but a calling down of a curse upon himself if he was not telling the truth (74). According to John, the third denial was precipitated by a relative of the man whose ear Peter had cut off; he asked, 'Did I not see you in the garden with him?' (John 18:26). That led others to join in and they pointed out his Galilean accent; Peter was a northener among southerners. His response was yet more virulent cursing, stopped by two things: the cock crowed, and Jesus, passing through the court, looked at him (Luke 22:61). Peter fled, burst into tears and sobbed his heart out.

Several questions arise from this incident. How did it happen that Peter let Jesus down so badly? Presumably because he had not thought carefully enough about what Jesus had said regarding the sufferings ahead of him and, as a corollary, he had not taken seriously what Jesus had said about the necessity of bearing a cross after him. But further: How did it happen that the church let Peter down so badly? Peter's denial is one of the few incidents to be recorded in all four Gospels! There is only one answer to that: *Peter* was the one who told what happened, with all the horrifying details. This he did for two reasons: to magnify the Lord who freely forgave him, as he does all who repent of their sin; and to urge Christians to do better than he did when called to account for their faith.

TO THINK ABOUT:
Beware of Peter's word, nor confidently say,
'I never will deny thee, Lord' – but – 'Grant I never may'.
Man's wisdom is to seek his strength in God alone;
And even an angel would be weak who trusted in his own.
                                                    (W. Cowper)

27:1–14 Jesus before Pilate, and the end of Judas

As the story of the anointing of Jesus was inserted between the account of the plot of the sanhedrin and Judas's approach to them (26:1–16), so the end of Judas is set between the report of the sanhedrin's meeting to formulate a charge and the appearance of Jesus before Pilate.

The meeting of the sanhedrin was called to secure a formal agreement on the charge against Jesus, since the governor alone could carry out a verdict for capital punishment (John 18:31). The charge was that Jesus claimed to be a king. Its full terms are recorded in Luke 23:2, where the allegation that Jesus forbade payment of tribute money to Caesar filled out what a Roman in Palestine would assume, that this 'king' set himself against Caesar's rule, as did the Zealots.

To Pilate's question, 'Are *you* the king of the Jews?' Jesus could say neither 'Yes' nor 'No'. 'Yes' would mean, as Pilate would hear it, that Jesus did claim to be ruler of the Jews over against Caesar, as the Jews alleged. 'No' would deny the authority of Jesus as representative of God's lordship over the Jews – as of the nations; hence he replied as he did to Caiaphas: 'You have said so', a qualified affirmative. To the further accusations of the chief priests and elders Jesus had nothing to say (12–14); one issue only was worthy of reply, his kingship, for that was from his Father (John 18:36).

The remorse of Judas in betraying innocent blood brought a contemptuous response from the chief priests; having confessed his sin he threw the money to the ground in the temple courts and went and hanged himself (3–5). Since the priests could not put the money into the treasury (on the basis of Deut. 23:18!), they bought the potter's field, for the burial of (Jewish) strangers who died in Jerusalem (as pilgrims). So, said Matthew, was fulfilled the prophecy contained in Zechariah 11:13 (not Jeremiah – a scribal slip of later times), with its curious alternative readings: the prophet, called of God to be shepherd of the flock, threw the thirty shekels of silver paid him as derisory wages 'to the treasury' (Hebrew, *ōtsar*), or 'to the potter' (Hebrew, *yōtser*). The incident was seen by Matthew as a type of the treatment of the Great Shepherd. Schlatter suggests that Christians viewed the purchase of the potter's field for thirty pieces of silver as a standing memorial of the ingratitude and unbelief of the people for the Shepherd God sent to them.

TO THINK ABOUT: The contrast between the end of Judas and the issue of Peter's denial in apostolic ministry: the difference between remorse and repentance is that between death and life.

27:15–31 A fateful choice

A Roman governor attended to his official business early in the morning. A crowd had gathered early this day to voice their choice of the one to whom Pilate should show clemency, among them, doubtless, many supporters of Barabbas. Mark informs us that Barabbas was an insurrectionist (Mark 15:7); having committed murder in an uprising he will have been of the Zealot persuasion. His name is intriguing. 'Barabbas' means 'Son of the Father'. Some authorities read it, 'Barabban', 'Son of the rabbi'. More importantly, some notable authorities give his name in 16, 17 as 'Jesus Barabbas'. If this last is correct the Jews are given the choice of 'Jesus Barabbas or Jesus who is called Christ' (17). What a contrast of champions of Israel! Jesus Barabbas, a deliverer through the sword that sheds blood of others, or Jesus Messiah, a saviour through the gift of his own life. The gathered crowd had no hesitation: the Messiah who preached love to God and neighbour and a kingdom of heaven for the poor in spirit was of little use to them: give them the man of blood!

Pilate's behaviour in this scene is entirely out of keeping with everything recorded of him. Why was this ruthless man so hesitant on this occasion? Two factors will have been operative: the impression made on him by Jesus (very clear in John's account); and the message sent by his wife (19). Like all Romans, Pilate will have known of the dream about blood which Calpurnia, Julius Caesar's wife had; if Caesar had listened to her he would have lived and not been murdered. Now his own wife has a comparable dream! Hence his vacillation and, at length, his endeavour to wash his hands free of the blood of 'this righteous man'. Matthew alone records the cry of the crowd in v. 25; by the time he wrote his Gospel their words had received a dreadful fulfilment in the blood-bath of Jerusalem in AD 70.

The treatment of Jesus by the soldiers was characteristic of Roman cruelty abroad. They had with them 'the king of the Jews'; accordingly they dressed him as Caesar, wove a wreath of thorns in imitation of the emperor's laurel wreath, provided him with a rod for a sceptre and greeted him with, 'Hail, King of the Jews!' in imitation of 'Hail, Caesar!' Then they beat him mercilessly. The more affecting is the prayer when rthese same men drove nails into the flesh of Jesus: 'Father, forgive them . . .'

A PRAYER: Whene'er in this wild world we meet
　　　　　Unkindly deeds that anger move,
　　　Teach us forgiveness – triumph sweet,
　　　　To conquer evil will with love.
　　　　　　　　　　(W. Romanis)

27:32–44 The crucifixion of Jesus

A story lies hidden in v. 32, which would be fascinating to unearth were it possible. Simon of Cyrene was 'coming in from the country', says Mark 15:21. A group of manuscripts in Matthew add the phrase, 'in order to meet him' (32). A condemned man had to carry his own cross (or cross-beam) to the place of execution; Jesus did so (John 19:17) till he could go no further; *that* was the point where Simon met him. He was ordered by the soldiers to follow Jesus, carrying his cross after him. One remembers another Simon who failed to carry a 'cross' for himself (Mark 8:34). Simon will have stood by the cross till the end – and was moved to love the man who died on it. As Mark gives the names of his sons (Mark 15:21) it is clear that the family became well known in the churches. Oddly enough, when gnostics tried to avoid the unpleasant fact that Jesus died, they alleged that Simon changed places with Jesus and was crucified in his place! That's an instance of a theology which deliberately twists history to make its own point.

Jesus was offered wine mingled with 'gall', says Matthew (34), doubtless with Psalm 69:21 in mind; Mark has 'myrrh', which was added with wine to make a stupefying drink and given by women to the crucified to lessen their pain. Jesus refused the wine; he would not offer himself for mankind in a stupefied state. Observe the extreme brevity of the description of the crucifixion in v. 35: it is reduced to two words in the Greek text, 'having-crucified him'! It's what took place between the Father and the Son that counted. For the soldiers' gambling for the clothes of Jesus, and its relation to Psalm 22:18, see John 19:23, 24.

It was usual for a condemned man to carry a notice, bearing his name and offence, and for it to be affixed to his cross. John 19:20–22 is of importance here: the title was written in languages for all the world to understand, and Pilate refused to alter the wording: Jesus dies as 'King of the Jews' – and of the world! This was celebrated in the version of Psalm 96:10 current in Latin churches: 'The Lord reigns *from the wood of the cross!*'

The mockers beside the cross have no idea how they fulfil the scriptures – and the purpose of God (compare Ps. 22:7–8). Their call to Jesus to step down from the cross was a last renewal of the temptations (compare Matt. 4:5–6).

TO THINK ABOUT:
Thou must have looked on Simon, turn, Lord, and look on me,
Till I shall see and follow, and bear thy cross for thee.

(H. R. Mackintosh)

27:45–54 The death of Jesus

From the sixth to the ninth hour (from midday to 3.00 p.m.) Jesus hung upon the cross and in that time there was an unnatural darkness (45). An eclipse of the sun is out of the question, since there was a full moon. It is likely to have been caused by a black sirocco, such as is common in Jerusalem in early April, though of a miraculous intensity (Lagrange). Spurgeon saw in this a parable of the impenetrable darkness of the mystery of the atonement – of what transpired between the Father and the Son in those terrible hours. The cry of Jesus in v. 46 is included in that mystery. It cites the opening words of Psalm 22, reflecting utter desolation of spirit of a man of God. As many have pointed out, to cite a scripture passage like a psalm is to recall the drift of the whole. Psalm 22 passes from an expression of forsakenness and rejection (1–18) through petition (19–21) to joyful confidence in God, who answers prayer and exalts his servants (22–31). The last cry of Jesus, referred to in v. 50 of our passage, is stated by John to be a triumphant 'It is finished!' (John 19:30), and that well summarises the mood of the end of Psalm 22. It would appear that Jesus experienced something essentially akin to that foreshadowed in the psalm, knowing the desolation of deprivation of the Father's fellowship, as he identified himself with mankind in its sin, but advancing to exultant confession of victory through the Father's grace. Jesus did not die in hopeless distress, but in the joyful consciousness of *victory*!

The rending of the curtain of the temple (between the 'holy place' and the 'most holy place') was acknowledged from earliest times as a sign from God that the way to his presence stands wide open through the death of his Son (compare Heb. 9:8 with 10:19–20). The portents of 51–53 have mystified exegetes through the centuries. A favourite view is that it is an echo of the release of the spirits in prison (see Eph. 4:9–10; 1 Pet. 3:19). Yet 52–53 are clearly linked with the resurrection of Jesus; their being placed at this point may be to show that Christ's atoning death leads to the fulfilment of God's covenant promise that his people shall participate in the first resurrection (Schlatter).

The confession of the centurion was not that of the church: 'This was *a son of God*' (54, compare Luke 23:47). But he uttered more than he knew. 'The Christian reader adds for himself, Yes: and other there is none' (B. W. Bacon).

TO THINK ABOUT: Friend, it is over now,
The passion, the sweat, the pains,
Only the truth remains.

(J. Masefield)

27:55–66 The burial of Jesus

The significant role played by women in the ministry of Jesus is maintained to the end: they stayed by the cross (55–56), watched at his tomb (61), were first at the tomb on Easter Sunday morning (28:1) and received the first resurrection appearances (first Mary, John 20:11–16, then the other women, Matt. 28:8–10).

The action of Joseph of Arimathea in requesting permission to bury Jesus was courageous; having disagreed with his fellow members of the sanhedrin about Jesus (Luke 23:51) he now embodied his dissent in action. To save Jesus from being buried in a public field as a criminal he gives him an honourable burial in his own new tomb. In this he was aided by Nicodemus (John 19:39).

The request of some chief priests and Pharisees the next day for a guard to be placed at the tomb of Jesus has been widely discussed. How should they have known that Jesus said, 'After three days I will rise again'? Matthew 12:39–40 supplies one occasion on which scribes and Pharisees were so addressed. The saying of Jesus about destroying the temple and in three days raising it was much chewed over at his trial (Matt. 26:61); it is the only accusation against him reported by the evangelists (note also the version in John 2:19). Moreover, the expression 'after three days' (or 'on the third day') occurs frequently in the Old Testament, always in connection with deliverance of some kind; these references are collected together in the Mishnah and they led to the dictum, 'The Holy One, blessed be he, never leaves the righteous in distress more than three days'. There is little doubt that the use of this expression by Jesus made some member of the sanhedrin uneasy and he communicated his feelings to others, hence the request of Pilate. The governor declined to use soldiers for such a purpose, so he told the Jews to use their own guard (65). So the sepulchre was sealed and a guard placed to keep intruders from breaking in. It never occurred to them to ask of what use they were in keeping the man within from bursting out!

FOR PRAISE:

Vainly they watch his bed,
  Jesus, my Saviour,
Vainly they seal the dead,
  Jesus, my Lord.

Death cannot keep his prey,
  Jesus, my Saviour,
He tore the bars away,
  Jesus, my Lord.

Up from the grave he arose!

28:1–15 The resurrection of the Lord

On Easter morning the women mentioned in 27:61 set out from home to perform the last acts of love on the body of Jesus. The scene that met them was beyond belief: the stone from the tomb was rolled away and a heavenly visitant was enthroned on it! The rolled-away stone and the empty tomb were signs that the Lord of life had been at work in re-creative power; in the raising of the saviour-Christ to power and glory he had anticipated the end of the world. The resurrection of Jesus meant the beginning of the new world, the opening of the kingdom of God for mankind. In him a new humanity stood in a new creation in which death had no power (see 2 Cor. 5:17 and 1 Cor. 15:20–23).

The announcement of the angel to the women included an invitation to examine the empty grave (6) and a command to tell the disciples the good news about the resurrection of Jesus, in particular that 'he is going before you to Galilee' (7). The same message is repeated when the Lord meets the women (10). Why mention a journey to Galilee at this point, when the disciples are still in Jerusalem and the Lord is to meet them there? As the scriptures give no answer on this point we can only guess. Just a few days earlier the disciples were looking for Jesus to inaugurate his kingdom in Jerusalem (Luke 19:11). When they grasp that Jesus is risen and has conquered his enemies – Caiaphas, Pilate, the Jews, the devil, and death itself – and that the resurrection for the kingdom has begun, what will their imaginations run to? They must learn *at once* that this is not the time for subjugating enemies and assuming thrones, but for gathering forces for mission to the world. This the Lord is to explain later – in Galilee! (18–20).

The reaction of the sanhedrin to the report of the guards shows two things: (1) the Jewish rulers remain in their unbelief, despite the resurrection; (2) it supplies the origin of the slander about the disciples stealing the body of Jesus, a slander circulating in Matthew's days, and still remaining in the Talmud.

TO THINK ABOUT: 'To preach the fact of the Resurrection was the first function of the evangelist, to embody the doctrine of the Resurrection is the great office of the Church; to learn the meaning of the Resurrection is the task not of one age only, but of all' (Bishop Westcott).

28:16–20 The commission of the risen Lord

One observation should be made about this passage. It is the only appearance of the risen Lord to the disciples recorded by Matthew. He will have known that there were many appearances, but has chosen to relate one only, and in it he has set a summary of the instruction the Lord gave in the resurrection. Naturally the summary is in his own language, but the content is the word of the risen Christ.

At the beginning of his account of the ministry, Matthew recorded the law of the Messiah from a mountain (chs. 5–7). Now the Lord gives, from a mountain, the commands which are to guide his church on its mission. That some 'doubted' does not necessarily imply the presence of others beside the apostles (some think that the 'more than five hundred brethren' were present, 1 Cor. 15:6). Matthew knows that disciples doubted Jesus in the resurrection appearances (compare Luke 24:37–41; John 20:24–29). As in the upper room (John 13–17) the disciples represent the church, so on the resurrection mountain.

Jesus begins with an affirmation: 'All authority in heaven and on earth has been given to me'. By his resurrection the Lord has assumed the throne with God, bringing about the first fulfilment of the vision of Daniel 7:13–14 where the Son of man is given 'dominion and glory and kingdom'. Since his authority extends over all nations and by his death he opened the kingdom for all nations, the disciples are sent to all nations. The extent of the church's mission is as wide as the scope of the Lord's redemption and rule.

The disciples are commanded to make disciples, baptise and teach. To make disciples assumes the proclamation of the gospel, with the call to repentance and faith; they confess him to be redeemer and Lord. Such are to be baptised 'in the name of' the Father, Son and Spirit; a formula expressing the idea of coming under the sovereignty of the triune God, for his glory and service. Having become servants of the Lord, disciples are to receive the instruction given by the Lord, given and received in the spirit of Matthew 11:28–30. By this means his disciples become the fellowship of the Father, Son and Spirit, heirs of the kingdom of God, and its continuing instrument in the world.

The Lord does not merely send; he comes with us as we go! (compare Mark 16:19–20).

A PRAYER:
Send forth thy gospel, holy Lord! Kindle in us love's sacred flame;
Love giving all and grudging nought for Jesus' sake, in Jesus' name.
(H. E. Fox)

Questions for further study and discussion on 26:69–28:20

1. In what circumstances is denial of Christ repeated in our life and how should we react to the recognition of such action?

2. What counterpart of the choice, 'Jesus or Barabbas', confronts today (i) the Jewish nation, (ii) the Gentile nations?

3. Muslims, like the gnostics, deny that Jesus was crucified; how will you enable them to grasp the truth when you meet them?

4. Pagans, like the Jews, deny that Jesus rose from death; how will you convince western, secular man of the truth of his resurrection?

5. Consider the implications of Matthew 28:18–20 for evangelistic methods today.